30-Minute Meals

SUSAN E. MITCHELL
Writer

JILL FOX
SALLY W. SMITH
Editors

LINDA HINRICHS
CAROL KRAMER
Designers

DAVID FISCHER
PATRICK LYONS
Photographers

BUNNY MARTIN
Food Stylist

CAROL HACKER
Photographic Stylist

Danielle Walker *(far left)* is chairman of the board and founder of the California Culinary Academy. **Susan E. Mitchell** *(left)* has worked as a chef and in recipe development, as a food consultant for restaurant and food companies, as a food stylist, and in product promotion for media tours. She is a graduate of the London Cordon Bleu School of Cooking, and holds a degree in home economics from Washington State University. She is the author of three cookbooks and many articles for food magazines and restaurant trade journals. Currently Ms. Mitchell writes, develops recipes, and works as a food consultant in Los Angeles, California.

The California Culinary Academy Among the forefront of American institutions leading the culinary renaissance in this country, the California Culinary Academy in San Francisco has gained a reputation as one of the most outstanding professional chef training schools in the world. With a teaching staff recruited from the best restaurants of Western Europe, the California Culinary Academy educates students from around the world in the preparation of classical cuisine. The recipes in this book were created in consultation with the chefs of the California Culinary Academy. For information about the Academy, write the Office of the Dean, California Culinary Academy, 625 Polk Street, San Francisco, CA 94102.

Front Cover

Meals made in 30 minutes need not be bland. Kiwi fruit from New Zealand adds color and zest to the Seafood Sauté menu on page 20. Also featured are Squash Medley and Watercress-and-Mushroom Salad With Poppy Seed Dressing.

Title Page

The Turkey Tonight menu on page 45 includes several topping variations for low-cost Turkey Breast Cutlets. Serve the Asparagus-and-Cheese variation when fresh asparagus is at its peak in late spring.

Back Cover

Upper left: Chicken breasts are ideal for a speedy sauté and a bit of kitchen showmanship. The Chicken for Company menu on page 32 features Chicken With Mushrooms coated in Madeira and ignited for a flambé finish.

Upper right: Four Cornish game hens are arranged artfully on a platter with baby carrots and green beans. Among the lessons to be learned from professional chefs is that the way food is presented is just as important as how it tastes.

Lower left: A rich veal stock of leeks, carrots, potatoes, onions, and herbs can be used in a variety of ways for everything from soup to sauces.

Lower right: The Spring Salmon Feast menu on page 26 is a light meal of pure simplicity. The placement of the Tomatoes au Gratin in the Broiled Salmon Steaks is a small but special touch. Fifty easy dinner menus begin on page 14.

Contributors

Contributing Writer
Rebecca Pepper

Calligrapher
Chuck Wertman

Consultant
Maggie Blyth Klein

Food and Wine Consultants
James R. Bartlett
Annette C. Fabri
Connie Krough-Wirt
Lorinda Moholt
Carolyn E. Petersen
Maureen Reynolds

Additional Photographers
Michael Lamotte, front cover; back cover: upper right and lower left; pages 13, 21, and 59
Laurie Black, Academy photography
Fischella, photograph of Danielle Walker

Additional Food Stylists
Karen Ray Gibson, assistant
Amy Nathan, front cover; back cover: upper right and lower left; pages 13, 21, and 59

Additional Photographic Stylists
Sara Slavin, front cover; pages 13, 21, and 59
Jeff Van Hanswyk, at the Academy

Editorial Staff
Beverley DeWitt
Don Mosley
Catherine Pearsall

Art and Production Staff
Linda Bouchard
Deborah Cowder
Lezlly Freier
Anne Pederson

Lithographed in U.S.A. by
Webcrafters, Inc.

The California Culinary Academy series is produced by the staff of Ortho Information Services.

Publisher
Robert L. Iacopi

Production Director
Ernie S. Tasaki

Series Managing Editor
Sally W. Smith

Address all inquiries to:
Ortho Information Services
Chevron Chemical Company
Consumer Products Division
575 Market Street
San Francisco, CA 94105

Copyright © 1986
Chevron Chemical Company
All rights reserved under international and Pan-American copyright conventions.

1 2 3 4 5 6 7 8 9
86 87 88 89 90 91

ISBN 0-89721-051-4

Library of Congress Catalog Card Number 85-073223

Chevron Chemical Company
575 Market Street, San Francisco, CA 94105

C O N T E N T S

30-Minute Meals

Any meal benefits from being served with style. With a variety of tablecloths, placemats, and napkins, one set of dishes can provide many looks.

Quick Cooking Basics

What is a 30-minute meal? Simple, fresh foods prepared with quick cooking techniques. Though time may be short, meals can still be fresh and delicious once you master the simple methods of cooking explained in this book. This chapter provides the beginnings—help with organizing your kitchen and your cooking, suggestions on which utensils and staples to have on hand, and directions for basic quick cooking techniques. Use these ideas to have some fun and to develop your own shortcuts, so you can spend less time cooking and more time enjoying great meals.

Getting out all the menu ingredients and doing your chopping, slicing, and mincing before you begin to cook is an important part of quick cooking. The ingredients for the Sunday Special menu (see page 34) are assembled here for efficient preparation.

HOW TO MAKE A 30-MINUTE MEAL

No cookbook has an answer for every situation. There will be nights when your idea of a quick meal is putting a roast and potatoes in the oven and lying down for an hour, or having someone else cook, or going to a restaurant, or skipping dinner entirely. But much of the time, you want to make a meal that's imaginative, tasty, and nutritious, without spending hours in the kitchen. This cookbook makes such meals possible via quick cooking techniques.

And what are these techniques?

1. Organizing the kitchen for efficiency.

2. Gathering all utensils and ingredients before doing anything else.

3. Chopping, slicing, and measuring all ingredients before actually beginning to cook.

4. Preparing several dishes at once, using quick cooking methods.

5. Serving and garnishing the meal in ways that add to its appeal.

The technique that makes the biggest difference and takes the most practice is cooking several dishes at once. If you're preparing a complete top-of-the-stove meal, you may have something going on all four burners. The first time you attempt this, it may feel as if the whole process might get away from you at any minute. But it won't, and as you cook more meals in this fashion, your skill will increase rapidly. Not only is this approach to cooking fun and satisfying, but you'll also impress your family and friends with your new-found culinary talents.

Gradually you'll be able to add even more flair to your cooking: keeping the kitchen neat and tidy while you whip up an incredible meal, carrying on a conversation without missing a beat, experimenting with garnishes, or directing a kitchen assistant or two and being ready to eat in no time at all.

The idea of the 30-minute timetable is *not* to become frazzled trying to "beat the clock," particularly at first. The best approach is to prepare the menus without constantly watching the clock—then if it has taken you more than 30 minutes, look for ways to cut down your time. One tester's first effort took 45 minutes, but as she became used to the techniques, her preparation times fell well within the 30-minute range. You'll also find that some menus can easily be prepared in less than 30 minutes—and that you'll need all the time for others.

Use the cooking plans to guide you in your first attempts at quick cooking. The philosophy behind them is simple: Begin with the dish that takes the longest to cook *and* that can wait the longest before serving. This generally means the starch (rice or potatoes) or a long-cooking vegetable. If the rice is done before the rest of the meal, simply turn off the heat and let it sit. The cooking plans also remind you to preheat the broiler or oven and to heat water for pasta or for steaming vegetables.

In cooking with this book, use your imagination and follow your own preferences. For instance, the side dishes given in the menus beginning on page 16 are suggestions only, not absolute musts. Keeping in mind color, texture, and flavor, substitute other vegetables or starches as you wish, using fresh produce whenever possible. (Of course, following the suggested menus can be a good way to introduce yourself and your family to unfamiliar foods and to new ways of preparing old favorites.)

Don't overlook the variations that accompany many of the menus. They increase entrée possibilities substantially. And you can also use sauces for one type of meat on another.

KITCHEN BASICS

Whether prepared in a leisurely fashion or in a rush, a good meal requires that the cook be organized. One way to be organized is to reduce the time it takes to put a meal on the table by fixing a casserole or a stew ahead of time, then heating it just before serving. Another way is to reduce the total cooking time by preparing the meal from scratch in just 30 minutes.

Both methods are effective. And the elements of organization involved in both methods are the same— efficient kitchen layout and storage, careful menu planning and shopping, a well-stocked pantry, and the appropriate cooking equipment.

Layout and Storage

Obviously, you don't have to remodel your kitchen to cook your meals in 30 minutes, but when you improve an awkward kitchen floor plan, you can make meal preparation a much more efficient process. Often it can be done quite simply. For instance, a movable chopping-block cart can reduce the number of steps you have to take and at the same time increase your usable counter space.

Take a few minutes to inventory the items you use most frequently— utensils, chopping blocks, spices, lids, oven mitts, and so on. Stand at your stove and your countertop preparation area and see if you really have easy access to all of them. If not, spend some time figuring out the best place to put them so that they'll be convenient. Do whatever you can to improve your storage, taking advantage of the many items now available: drawer dividers; containers for storing utensils by the stove; and wall, door, and ceiling racks. Having what you need close at hand saves more time than you may realize.

Menu Planning and Shopping

The idea of menu planning is to ensure that when you start cooking, you have everything you need right at hand. It might seem that detailed planning will eliminate flexibility or spontaneity, but you should find that you can be more creative by planning ahead—you won't get stuck with yet another tuna casserole because you don't have the ingredients for something special in the house. Once you get into the habit of planning menus several days to a week ahead, you'll find you're more relaxed because everything is under control. You'll also cut grocery bills and save time.

One method some people like for speeding up shopping is this: Type up a basic list in an order that reflects the layout of your supermarket and the route you generally take through it. Make photocopies of the list and post them in a convenient place in the kitchen. As you run short of the items on the list, check them off on the top copy. Add items from the menus you have planned and you have your shopping list. Also, post menus and check each morning for foods that need defrosting.

Staples

A good supply of staple items gives you options. Many of the pasta- or rice-based main dishes and the soup-and-sandwich meals in this book can be made from staples; they are perfect for nights when you don't feel like cooking what you had planned. Staples means more than just salt, flour, sugar, and milk. To prepare the 30-minute menus, you'll need to have many of the items on the following list. Don't forget family favorites.

Precooked Chicken Frozen in meal-sized quantities, precooked chicken makes a speedy dinner entrée or salad. Stewing a whole chicken or two is simple, economical, and takes little attention.

7

Stock After cooking a chicken, freeze the stock in an ice tray, for individual cubes, or in larger containers. Keep canned chicken and beef broth in your pantry to use full strength in soups, as a base for sauces, or to add flavor to rice or pilafs. Bottled clam juice can be used in much the same way beef or chicken broth is.

Canned or Frozen Seafood Shrimp, crabmeat, salmon, and tuna are handy to use as additions to omelets, pasta, soup, and salads.

Pâtés and Cold Cuts These are useful for sandwiches, hors d'oeuvres, omelets, and salads.

Fresh Vegetables Keep a plentiful supply of fresh onions, garlic, and potatoes on hand. Carrots keep well enough to qualify as a staple, too.

Canned Vegetables In all but the summer months, canned tomatoes (whole and stewed) are generally more flavorful than fresh. Also keep canned tomato or vegetable juice cocktail available to flavor sauces.

Frozen Vegetables Frozen peas are a quick way to add interest to pasta, entrées, and salads. Because they freeze in a solid block, peas in boxes must be cooked before they can be used; the bags are handier because the peas stay separate, so you can take out any amount. Mincing onion in quantity saves time; freeze it in quarter-cupfuls.

Fresh Fruits You'll need fresh citrus fruits for juice and for garnishes.

Dried, Canned, and Frozen Fruits Especially during the winter months, stock these items for quick desserts and breakfasts, and to add to dinner entrées. A selection of frozen and bottled fruit juices, including lemon and lime, is also useful.

Milk For dinner sauces, soups, and desserts, stock whipping cream (or its low-calorie substitute, evaporated skim milk), yogurt, sour cream, non-fat dry milk, and ice cream or sherbet.

Cheeses You'll find many uses for Monterey jack, Cheddar, Parmesan or Romano, and low-calorie ricotta. Grate hard cheese in quantity and store in a container in the freezer; it will not freeze solid.

Eggs Try to keep hard-cooked eggs on hand; you'll use them for salads, sandwich fillings, and garnishes.

Pasta and Rice Pasta—in its many assorted sizes, shapes, and colors—and rice can always be turned into a quick meal.

Cereals Of course, you'll use them for breakfast, but they can also contribute to cookies and parfaits.

Baked Goods Frozen tortillas, crêpes, and croissants let you create quick entrées or out-of-the-ordinary breakfasts and lunches. Cookies and poundcake provide quick dessert possibilities, and they, too, freeze well.

Bread Crumbs Keep them on hand for crunchy toppings and coatings.

Fresh Flavorings Fresh herbs, which have more flavor than dried, can be stored in water in the refrigerator. Some of the most frequently used ones are parsley, watercress, cilantro, basil, oregano, dill, chives, and rosemary. You can also store garlic in the refrigerator for up to a month: mince, cover with oil, and store tightly capped. Sprigs of fresh herbs make attractive garnishes.

Dried Flavorings A well-stocked shelf of dried spices and herbs will tide you over when you cannot obtain them fresh.

Frozen Flavorings Well-wrapped ginger root can be frozen indefinitely. Many herbs can also be frozen when in season.

Canned and Bottled Flavorings You should have vegetable and olive oil; vinegars (red and white wine, cider, and herb); Worcestershire, hot-pepper, and soy sauce; Dijon mustard; and Mexican salsa. For desserts and special breakfasts, stock syrups—maple, berry, and chocolate. For toppings, keep bittersweet chocolate, nuts, raisins, and grated coconut.

Wines and Liqueurs Entrées may be flavored with sherry, Madeira, Marsala, Cognac, or brandy, or with the red or white wine to be served with the dinner. Liqueurs such as Grand Marnier, Cointreau, amaretto, and Frangelica add their distinct tastes to desserts—and create a dramatic effect when flamed.

Equipment

To prepare 30-minute meals, you don't have to have a pressure cooker, microwave oven, convection oven, slow cooker, blender, or food processor. But they are time-savers that can be a big help. Information on adapting standard techniques to microwave cooking can be found on page 12.

To prepare the menus in this book, however, you *will* need the following (identified by number in the photograph on the facing page):

1. Large skillets with lids—one or two 8- or 10-inch.

2. Large and small frying pans—two 12-inch, heavy-bottomed, with slanted sides; one 6-inch.

3. Small and medium saucepans with lids—1- or 1½-quart; 2½- or 3-quart.

4. Large pot with lid—6-quart or larger.

5. Shallow baking dish—1½- or 2-quart for casseroles.

6. Heavy baking sheets—two.

7. Steamer—perforated insert that fits the pot or saucepan.

8. Ovenproof serving platter—a shallow casserole can be substituted.

9. Knives—one of each:

  a. 10- to 12-inch chopping knife, heavy steel;

  b. serrated bread knife;

  c. 6½- to 8-inch utility knife, stainless steel with thin, slender blade;

  d. 3- or 4-inch paring knife.

10. Polyethylene or wood chopping boards—small, for garlic and onions; large, for everything else.

11. Mallet—for pounding cutlets.

12. Colander; medium strainer; vegetable peeler; lemon/lime juicer; and four-sided, stainless-steel grater.

13. Measuring cups and spoons—liquid and dry.

14. Spatulas—metal and rubber.

15. Long-handled spoons—regular and slotted.

16. Large and small whisks.

17. Stainless-steel mixing bowls—in assorted sizes.

18. Electric hand mixer.

19. Mortar and pestle.

Optional, but nice to have:

  Tongs
  Long-handled fork
  Hard-cooked egg slicer
  Tomato wedger
  Butter molds
  Mushroom brush
  Dredger
  Small grater
  Serrated fruit knife with curved end
  Apple corer
  Poultry shears
  Individual casserole dishes
  Blender, food processor
  Toaster oven

Equipping your kitchen for a variety of cooking needs does not have to be an expensive endeavor, nor take up a great deal of storage space. Prepare any of the 30-minute menus, which begin on page 16, with just the basic equipment shown here. Descriptions of these items begin on the facing page.

PREPARING TO COOK

What you do before you turn on the stove is at least as important as your proficiency at cooking. First, read the recipes and the cooking plan for the menu to familiarize yourself with the instructions and the overall process. Then gather everything you will need—ingredients, equipment and utensils, cutting board, and serving platters. It's tempting to ignore this step (after all, it will only take a second to get out the measuring cup), but don't be fooled. Finding things while you're cooking takes more time than you think. It took one tester more than three minutes just to locate the whisk when he needed it.

Preparation also includes measuring, chopping, and mincing. This is what enables you to cook a number of dishes at one time. Keep the following preparation tips in mind:

☐ Invest in good-quality knives, keep them sharp, and store them properly.

☐ Use a cutting board large enough to accommodate your ingredients. The polyethylene ones now available are lightweight, can be scrubbed with soap and water with no ill effects, and can even be washed in the dishwasher.

☐ For safe, efficient slicing, begin by cutting in such a way as to create a flat side. Then turn the item flat side down and you'll be able to make slices without having it slip around.

☐ For mincing or chopping, use the professional chef's technique: keeping the point of the knife stationary, lift the handle up and down and pivot it from side to side.

☐ If more than one item will be added to a dish at the same time and all must be minced, do them all at once.

☐ When slicing or trimming vegetables such as celery, carrots, or beans, do three or four stalks or pieces at a time.

QUICK COOKING METHODS

As noted on page 6, the quick-cooking approach includes the ability to juggle a number of dishes at once. This is where familiarity with the recipes and cooking plan pays off—in facility at moving from one dish to another, checking, adding, and stirring. The main thing to keep in mind is that *you* are directing the action. If something seems to be cooking too fast, reduce the heat. If it takes you longer to complete a step than you thought it would, slow down other dishes that are already under way. Gradually, the timing will become natural to you and you won't have to keep referring to the cooking plan. And remember, if you're not used to cooking this way, trying to do so while keeping dinner guests entertained is not the best way to start. Either put them to work or try your first 30-minute meal when you can concentrate on what you're doing.

Most of the recipes in this book call for thin meat or poultry cutlets, fish fillets or small whole fish, ground meats, and chops. Some are heated and partly cooked on top of the stove and then placed in a hot oven to finish cooking or to brown. Most are cooked by one of the following methods:

Sautéing The sauté method—cooking thin, tender pieces of meat, fish, and vegetables in a little oil and butter over high heat—seals in both flavor and juices. For perfect sautéed foods that are not greasy, keep these points in mind:

☐ Use a mixture of butter and oil; oil helps butter withstand high temperatures without burning. If cholesterol is a concern, omit the butter. The flavor of the food will be a bit different, but the sauce will generally mask this.

☐ The butter and oil must be hot (but not smoking) when the food is added to the pan. This will quickly sear the food, forming the golden-brown surface characteristic of sautéed foods.

☐ Overcooking will toughen meats and poultry and cause fish and many vegetables to fall apart. If you are using frozen fish, be sure it is completely thawed (and drained and patted dry) before you sauté it. Otherwise, it will be watery and may not be completely cooked in the center. Poaching is a better choice for partially thawed fish.

☐ For foods as thin as ¼ inch, you should generally sauté no more than 5 minutes per side.

☐ For calves' liver, boned chicken or turkey breast slices, and thin fish fillets, a cooking time as short as 3 minutes per side can be sufficient.

☐ When the edges of a piece of food begin to curl, it is usually ready to be turned.

☐ Cooking times are given in all the recipes, but develop your judgment as to when foods are cooked to your liking.

Broiling Broiling—cooking under high heat without added fat—is also speedy and best for meat or fish that is more than ¼ inch thick.

☐ To obtain a browned exterior without overcooking the interior, the broiler must be hot (at 550° F) when foods are put under it. The cooking plans remind you to preheat the broiler in time for it to reach the proper temperature.

☐ To keep dry-fleshed fish or meats with little fat from drying out, brush with melted butter or oil before broiling.

☐ Generally, broil 1-inch-thick meat a minimum of 4 inches from the heat source. The thicker the piece, the further from the heat it should be placed—and the longer it will take to cook.

Poaching Poaching—gently simmering fish, seafood, poultry, or vegetables in seasoned liquid—is a low-calorie way of preparing food. For best results, the poaching liquid (water, wine, fish or chicken stock) should be hot when the food is added to it. Then reduce the heat and cook until the food is just tender.

Steaming Vegetables retain more nutrients and flavor and require little attention when steamed. The recipes in this book use two methods—steaming over rapidly boiling water and steaming in butter and water. The cooking times in this book produce tender-crisp vegetables.

☐ To steam vegetables over boiling water, use a metal steamer designed for the purpose, or substitute a colander. Place it over a few inches of water in a 2- or 3-quart saucepan with a tight-fitting lid.

☐ When the water boils, add the vegetables. Steaming will take from 5 to 20 minutes.

☐ To butter-steam, melt butter in a large skillet over medium-high heat. Add the vegetables and about ¼ inch of water, stir, cover tightly, and steam until vegetables are tender. Butter-steaming is an excellent method for long, thin vegetables such as asparagus or whole green beans. It's also a very quick way to cook cut-up vegetables, because the skillet offers a large surface area over which to spread them. The butter flavors the vegetables as they cook.

Preparing four items at once is easier when the ingredients are chopped and ready before cooking begins. Here, the elements of the Sunday Special menu (page 34) near simultaneous completion: the Broccoli Sauté (top left), the almonds (top right), the Savory Rice Pilaf (bottom right), and the Breast of Chicken à la Reimann entrée (bottom left).

THE MICROWAVE AND 30-MINUTE MEALS

Although a microwave oven cannot sauté or broil meats, it can be used for other cooking tasks in these 30-minute meals and has certain advantages. It provides another place to cook, can speed cleanup time by allowing you to cook and serve in the same dish, and can be used to warm bread or rolls without heating up the kitchen. It also conserves nutrients, particularly water-soluble vitamins, and saves energy.

The following hints assume the microwave is operating on 100% power; check your owner's manual to be sure this power and the times given are correct for your microwave.

☐ To cook **chicken breasts** for use in salads, soups, or fillings for crêpes and other entrées, place 1 half breast in a covered casserole with ¼ cup vermouth or chicken broth and ¼ cup chopped green onion. Microwave for 8 to 10 minutes. Cool breast and cut up.

☐ For the calorie-conscious, 1 pound of **fish** steams moist and tender in its own juices in 5 to 6 minutes. It tastes as if it were poached.

☐ **Fresh vegetables,** cut as directed in these recipes, take almost as long to cook in a microwave (including standing time) as when they are sautéed or steamed on top of the stove. But using the microwave frees the stove, and the vegetables will need little attention. To save time, use the microwave for steaming a vegetable before purée-ing or before a final sauté.

☐ A pound of most **vegetables,** cut in pieces of even size, will cook in 7 minutes. Root vegetables take 2 to 3 minutes more; very tender vegetables such as snow peas, 2 to 3 minutes less. Add little or no water and cook vegetables covered. Shake or stir once during cooking. Allow to stand 3 minutes after removing from microwave, to finish cooking internally.

☐ Warm a **lemon or lime** for 30 seconds before squeezing; you will get more juice.

☐ To toast ½ cup **almonds,** melt 1 tablespoon butter, add almonds, and microwave 2 minutes, stirring occasionally.

☐ Heat **brandy or other liqueurs** for flamed entrées and desserts for 15 to 30 seconds. Pour over dish and ignite.

☐ To warm **syrups** for waffles or pancakes, heat in a pitcher for 1 to 1½ minutes.

☐ Heat **bread and rolls** in a serving basket until warm to the touch; they will be hot inside.

☐ Use the microwave to simplify preparation of staples; it can dry bread cubes for **crumbs or croutons** (4 cups cubes, ⅓ cup melted butter, and choice of seasonings; cook on 100% power for 8 to 10 minutes, stirring occasionally) and can dry fresh **herbs** (microwave ½ cup leaves between paper towels 2 minutes).

☐ A bonus: With a microwave, you can add **baked potatoes** to 30-minute meals. Cook 4 to 5 minutes and then let rest, wrapped in a towel or aluminum foil, another 5 minutes to finish cooking. Flesh will be fluffy and moist but skin will not be crisp.

SERVING AND GARNISHING FOODS

Quick cooking is both fun in itself and the means to an end—enjoying relaxed, tasty, *attractive* meals. China, silver, and candles aren't the only ways to dress up a table. And you don't need three or four sets of dishes to have variety at mealtime. Use less expensive items like placemats, napkins, and a few coordinated tablecloths to create different moods. Find

small ways to make your table look special every night—and to change its appearance from week to week. Switch from a tablecloth to placemats or vice versa. Even a change of napkins makes a difference. Use small blooming plants—primroses, violets, crocus—or fragrant herbs as decorations; place the pots in colorful woven baskets or cover them with napkins. Changes such as new wine or water glasses or a set of flatware with colorful plastic handles are simple, inexpensive ways to give your table a new look. Unusual serving bowls, platters, and pitchers do the same. The photographs throughout this book should give you many new ideas—you'll see how the same dishes can be coordinated with a variety of table coverings to make them seem new and different.

The way in which the food itself is presented—arrangement, color, texture—really does affect its taste. If served with style, even the simplest food seems more flavorful. Good restaurants know this, and use it to their advantage—especially in garnishing foods for eye appeal. Garnishes can be complicated or simple, but they all whet the appetite and provide color contrast and textural interest. Cut in a variety of shapes, many vegetables and fruits are pretty as well as edible additions to any plate, and nuts, cheese, and other dairy products add both texture and flavor as toppings.

The garnishes and toppings listed below are some examples that are easy to prepare and add appeal to any menu.

☐ **Nuts** Almonds, slivered, sliced, and whole toasted; pecans; walnuts

☐ **Fresh fruits** Orange, lemon, and lime wedges and wheels; kiwi rounds; nectarine, peach, and pineapple slices; citrus segments; melon balls; whole berries, cherries, and grapes; citrus twists and grated rind; shredded coconut

- □ **Preserved and dried fruits and vegetables** Pickles, hot or mild chile peppers, dates, raisins, olives

- □ **Fresh herbs** Sprigs of basil, oregano, rosemary, thyme, watercress, parsley, dill, mint, cilantro

- □ **Cheese** Shredded Cheddar, Swiss, Monterey jack; grated Parmesan

- □ **Dairy products** Yogurt, sour cream, whipped cream, *crème fraîche*

- □ **Croutons** Plain and flavored; bread crumbs

- □ **Flavored butters** Citrus, nut, herb, maple

- □ **Eggs** Hard-cooked egg slices and sieved hard-cooked yolk

- □ **Vegetables** Whole and chopped green or red onion; scallion fans; fluted mushroom caps; mushroom slices; cherry tomatoes, whole and halves; tomato wedges and slices; carrot curls, sticks, and rounds; cucumber slices and twists; celery sticks; whole and sliced radishes and radish roses; avocado slices

- □ **Flowers** Petals or blossoms such as violets and nasturtiums—be sure they have not been sprayed

- □ **Candy** Chocolate curls and grated chocolate; candied violets

Attractive garnishes and tasty toppings take a few minutes to prepare, but they add a touch of elegance to everyday meals and simple foods.

13

Sautéing is a basic quick cooking method. A nutritious meal, such as this sautéed shrimp, can be ready to eat half an hour after you arrive home from work.

50 Easy Dinners

This chapter contains 50 dinner menus designed for quick cooking. They run the gamut from simple family fare to more elegant (and sometimes more expensive) meals that you might serve to company. For easy selection, the menus are arranged by the type of entrée—fish, poultry, veal, beef, liver, pork, lamb, pasta, skillet casserole, and salad, soup, and sandwich. All the recipes serve four adults. You can increase or reduce the ingredients to suit the appetites of your diners. Note, however, that if you're cooking for more than four, preparation may well take more than 30 minutes.

ELEGANT SOLE DINNER

*Sole With Lemon-Butter
Sauce and Grapes*

Savory Rice

Zucchini Sauté

*Wine suggestion:
Johannisberg Riesling*

*Sole and green grapes are
featured in this sautéed
entrée. Try substituting other
types of fish for the sole (keep
in mind that thicker fillets
will have to cook longer).
This simple technique lends
itself to many variations; try
the others given here. The
Savory Rice will be best with
saffron, but you can use
turmeric if necessary.*

COOKING PLAN

1. *Assemble all ingredients and
cooking equipment.*

2. *Start rice.*

3. *Wash grapes and mince parsley
for fish. Slice zucchini; mince parsley
and fresh basil. Mix seasoned flour.*

4. *Sauté zucchini.*

5. *Warm platter for fillets in 200° F
oven.*

6. *Coat fillets and sauté.*

7. *Remove fillets to platter and
prepare sauce.*

To Serve *Fluff rice. Pour sauce over
fillets and season zucchini.*

SOLE WITH LEMON-BUTTER SAUCE AND GRAPES

> 1¼ pounds sole fillets
> ½ cup flour seasoned with
> ¼ teaspoon salt and ⅛
> teaspoon pepper
> 1 tablespoon each *butter and oil*
> ¼ cup each *butter, lemon juice,
> and minced parsley*
> 1 cup seedless grapes

1. Dredge fillets in seasoned flour.
Warm serving platter.

2. In a large frying pan over medium-high heat, melt the 1 tablespoon
butter with the oil. Add as many of
the fillets as will fit, rounded side
first, and sauté until they turn a deep
golden color (about 1½ minutes per
side). Remove to platter and place in
oven. Repeat with remaining fillets.

3. Wipe out pan, return to heat, and
add the ¼ cup butter. When it is light
brown, add lemon juice, parsley, and
grapes. Swirl to heat grapes (1 minute) and pour sauce over fish.

Fillets Amandine Complete steps 1
and 2. Wipe out pan. Melt 1 tablespoon butter in pan. Add 2 to 3
tablespoons sliced almonds and sauté
until golden. Add 2 to 3 tablespoons
dry vermouth, white wine, or Marsala
and heat briefly. Pour over fillets.

Parmesan Fillets With Bananas
For step 1, dredge fillets in ¼ cup
each flour and freshly grated Parmesan cheese. Continue as directed in
step 2. Wipe out pan. Melt 2 tablespoons butter in pan, add 2 bananas,
sliced, and sauté them until heated
through. Add 1 tablespoon *each* lemon juice and minced parsley, heat,
and spoon over fillets.

Dilled Fillets With Cucumber
Complete steps 1 and 2. Wipe out
pan. Remove peel in alternate strips
from an English or a regular cucumber; slice cucumber thinly. Melt 2 to
3 tablespoons butter in pan. Add cucumber and 1 tablespoon fresh *or*
1 teaspoon dried dillweed; sauté until
warmed through. Spoon over fillets.

Fillets Provençale Complete steps
1 and 2. Wipe out pan. Melt 2 to
3 tablespoons butter in pan. Add
2 cloves garlic, minced; 1 zucchini,
thinly sliced; and 1 ripe tomato,
chopped. Sauté 5 to 7 minutes. Sprinkle ¼ teaspoon dried basil over surface and stir. Spoon over fillets.

Fillets With Herbed Yogurt Complete steps 1 and 2. Mix together ½
cup low-fat yogurt; 2 tablespoons dry
white wine; 1 egg yolk; 1 green
onion, chopped; 1 clove garlic,
minced; 3 tablespoons minced parsley; and ¼ teaspoon *each* dried
thyme, basil, and oregano. Heat
through and spread over fillets.

SAVORY RICE

> 2 cups water
> 1 cup white rice
> ½ teaspoon salt
> Pinch saffron or ⅛ teaspoon
> turmeric
> Minced parsley (*for garnish*)

Bring water, rice, salt, and saffron to
a boil. Cover, reduce heat, and simmer until all water is absorbed (20
minutes). Garnish with parsley.

ZUCCHINI SAUTÉ

> 2 tablespoons each *butter
> and oil*
> 1 pound zucchini, sliced
> ⅛ inch thick
> 2 cloves garlic, minced
> 2 tablespoons minced fresh
> parsley
> 1 tablespoon minced fresh *or*
> ½ to 1 teaspoon dried basil
> Salt and freshly ground
> pepper

1. In a large skillet over medium-
high heat, melt butter with oil. When
drops of water dance in the pan, add
zucchini, garlic, parsley, and basil.

2. Sauté, shaking skillet and tossing
slices gently with a spatula, until
tender-crisp (7 minutes). Season to
taste with salt and pepper.

QUICK CALAMARI DINNER

Calamari Steak Sauté

Sauced Spaghetti Squash

Butter-Steamed Green Beans

Wine suggestion:
Australian Cabernet Rosé

Calamari (squid) steaks take only about a minute to cook. Teamed with spaghetti squash topped with your favorite sauce, and green beans steamed with butter, they make a light, satisfying dinner. You can also serve the calamari with any of the sauces on page 16.

COOKING PLAN

1. Assemble all ingredients and cooking equipment.

2. Heat water for squash; quarter, seed, and begin to cook.

3. Warm spaghetti sauce over low heat.

4. Wash and slice beans, grate cheese, mince parsley, and slice lemon.

5. Mix seasoned flour and coat calamari steaks.

6. Butter-steam beans.

7. Preheat oven to 200° F.

8. Sauté calamari steaks; keep warm in oven.

9. Drain squash and shred.

To Serve *Top squash with sauce and parsley; accompany with cheese. Garnish calamari steaks with lemon, and serve beans.*

CALAMARI STEAK SAUTÉ

    1 to 1½ pounds calamari steaks
    ½ cup flour seasoned with
       ⅛ teaspoon each *dried
       basil, thyme,* and *oregano*
    1 *egg,* lightly beaten with
       2 tablespoons milk
    ½ cup bread crumbs
    2 tablespoons each *butter*
       and *oil*
       Lemon wheels (for garnish)

1. Coat steaks with seasoned flour, then with egg-milk mixture, and finally with bread crumbs.

2. Preheat oven to 200° F. In a wide frying pan, heat butter and oil. Add calamari steaks, without crowding pan, and sauté 30 to 35 seconds per side. Add butter as needed.

3. Garnish with lemon wheels.

SAUCED SPAGHETTI SQUASH

    1 spaghetti squash (about 4 lbs)
    1 jar (15½ oz) or 2 cups
       favorite spaghetti sauce
       Minced parsley (for garnish)
       Parmesan cheese

1. Wash squash and cut into quarters. Remove seeds.

2. Place in a large, covered pot in boiling water to cover, reduce heat to medium-high, and cook until tender (20 minutes). Drain.

3. Remove pulp from rind.

4. Top with heated sauce and parsley; serve with cheese.

BUTTER-STEAMED GREEN BEANS

    1 pound green beans
    2 tablespoons butter
    5 tablespoons water
       Salt and pepper

1. Wash and trim beans; slice diagonally into 1-inch lengths.

2. In a large skillet over medium-high heat, melt butter. Add beans and water, stir, cover, and steam until tender (7 minutes). Season to taste.

SEAFOOD SAUTÉ

Seafood With Kiwi

Squash Medley

*Watercress-and-Mushroom Salad
With Poppy Seed Dressing*

*Wine suggestion:
Chenin Blanc*

In the eye-catching entrée of this menu, the sweet taste of kiwi fruit and the tartness of lemon offer a tantalizing contrast to the delicate seafood. Other fruits, such as nectarines, papayas, or mangoes, can be substituted for the kiwi, if you wish. You might also want to add poppy or sesame seed rolls (warm them in a 350° F oven for 10 minutes).

COOKING PLAN

1. *Assemble all ingredients and cooking equipment.*

2. *Cut up squash, mince garlic and parsley, and grate cheese. Make salad and dressing.*

3. *Mince, chop, and slice ingredients for seafood dish.*

4. *Sauté seafood.*

5. *Sauté squash.*

6. *Add kiwi to seafood and make sauce.*

To Serve *Dress salad. Garnish seafood with lemon and squash with cheese and parsley.*

SEAFOOD WITH KIWI

> 2 tablespoons each *butter and oil*
> 1 to 3 cloves garlic, *minced or pressed*
> ½ to ¾ pound *cleaned raw medium-sized shrimp*
> ¾ pound halibut, *cut in 1-inch pieces*
> 2 *kiwi fruit, peeled and sliced*
> ¼ cup each *lemon juice and minced fresh parsley*
> 1 *lemon wheel, sliced in half (for garnish; optional)*

1. In a large frying pan over medium heat, melt butter with oil. Add garlic, shrimp, and halibut; sauté until shrimp just begin to turn pink and halibut becomes opaque (4 minutes).

2. Push seafood to edges of pan and warm kiwi briefly in center.

3. Combine lemon juice and parsley and gently mix with seafood.

4. Garnish with lemon wheel, if desired.

Fillets With Fruit Substitute 1 to 1½ pounds fillets of any white fish for the shrimp and halibut. Follow step 1, sautéing 2 to 4 minutes per side. In step 2, substitute 2 nectarines, sliced; 1 papaya, sliced; or segments of 1 orange and 1 grapefruit for the kiwi. Complete steps 3 and 4.

SQUASH MEDLEY

> 3 medium *zucchini squash*
> 3 medium *yellow crookneck squash*
> 2 tablespoons *butter*
> 1 or 2 cloves garlic, *minced or pressed*
> *Freshly grated Parmesan cheese and minced parsley (for garnish)*

1. Rinse and dry squash, and cut into large julienne.

2. In a large skillet over medium-high heat, melt butter. Add garlic and sauté until golden.

3. Add squash and sauté, tossing with a spatula to cook evenly (2 to 3 minutes).

4. Garnish with cheese and parsley before serving.

WATERCRESS-AND-MUSHROOM SALAD WITH POPPY SEED DRESSING

> 4 large or 8 medium *mushrooms, sliced*
> *Half a small red onion, sliced and separated into rings*
> 1 bunch *watercress, tough stems removed*

Poppy Seed Dressing

> ¼ cup each *honey and lemon juice*
> ¾ cup *walnut or safflower oil*
> 1 tablespoon *Dijon mustard*
> 1 green onion, *minced*
> 1 tablespoon *poppy seed*
> ½ teaspoon *salt*

Arrange mushrooms and onion rings on a bed of watercress. Top with Poppy Seed Dressing.

Poppy Seed Dressing Thoroughly combine honey, lemon juice, oil, mustard, onion, poppy seed, and salt.

Menu

**SEAFOOD SUPPER
ALL'ITALIANA**

Italian-Style Sea Bass

Spinach Pasta

*Wine suggestion:
Gamay Rosé or French Tavel*

For a light late-summer meal, try Italian-Style Sea Bass, baked in a sauce of garlic, pepper, onion, and tomato that also tastes good on the Spinach Pasta. If you like, add a simple salad of cucumbers and cherry tomatoes with an oil-and-vinegar dressing.

COOKING PLAN

1. *Assemble all ingredients and cooking equipment.*

2. *Preheat oven to 350° F.*

3. *Wash and chop vegetables for the fish.*

4. *Prepare sauce for fish, assemble dish, and put in oven.*

5. *Start water for pasta.*

6. *Add pasta to boiling water.*

7. *Check fish; if it flakes easily, it is done.*

8. *Check pasta; when it is al dente, drain.*

To Serve *Remove fish from oven and spoon some of the sauce over the pasta.*

ITALIAN-STYLE SEA BASS

You can substitute fillets of perch, flounder, snapper, or turbot for the sea bass in this dish.

> 1 tablespoon olive oil
> 1 clove garlic, minced
> ¼ cup each *seeded and chopped green pepper and chopped onion*
> 1 can (8 oz) tomatoes
> 1 tablespoon lemon juice
> 1 tablespoon chopped fresh or 1 teaspoon dried basil or oregano
> 4 sea bass fillets (1 to 1½ lbs fish)

1. Preheat oven to 350° F.

2. In a medium frying pan, heat oil. Add garlic, pepper, and onion and sauté until softened. Add tomatoes (breaking up with a fork) and their juice, lemon juice, and basil and heat through.

3. Place fillets in single layer in a shallow oven-to-table baking dish. Pour the sauce over the fish and cover with foil.

4. Bake until fish flakes easily at the touch of a fork (15 to 20 minutes).

SPINACH PASTA

> 2 quarts water
> 1 teaspoon salt
> 8 ounces green (spinach) pasta
> 1 tablespoon oil

1. In a large pot bring the water and salt to a boil.

2. Add pasta and oil and cook, uncovered, until pasta is al dente (5 to 8 minutes for medium-width noodles). Drain.

3. Spoon some of the fish sauce over pasta before serving.

22

MEXICAN FISH FIESTA

Mexicali Fish

Lemon-Lime Rice

Spicy Mexican Corn

Beverage suggestion:
Mexican beer

For a meal with south-of-the border flavor, try this menu. Fish fillets topped with almonds, cilantro, and a tangy sauce are wrapped in foil and baked while refreshing Lemon-Lime Rice and Spicy Mexican Corn cook on top of the stove.

COOKING PLAN

1. *Assemble all ingredients and cooking equipment.*

2. *Preheat oven to 450° F.*

3. *Start rice.*

4. *Juice lime and prepare sauce for fish.*

5. *Begin cooking corn.*

6. *Assemble fish packets and place in oven.*

7. *Add remaining ingredients to corn.*

8. *Measure or squeeze juice and mince parsley for rice. Cut lime into wedges for fish.*

9. *Check fish; if it flakes easily, it is done.*

To Serve *Add juice and parsley to rice. Open fish packets and garnish with lime. Serve corn.*

MEXICALI FISH

> *Juice of 1 lime*
> 1 *tablespoon cornstarch*
> ⅓ *cup white wine, clam juice, or water*
> 4 *snapper, cod, sea bass, or sole fillets (1 to 1½ lbs fish)*
> *Several sprigs of cilantro*
> ¼ *to ⅓ cup sliced almonds*
> 1 *lime, cut in wedges (for garnish)*

1. Preheat oven to 450° F. In a small saucepan mix lime juice and cornstarch. Stirring in wine, cook over medium-high heat until thickened.

2. Place each fillet on a piece of foil large enough to wrap it completely. Top with 1 or 2 sprigs of cilantro and one fourth of the almonds.

3. Divide sauce among fillets. Wrap packets, folding edges to seal, and arrange on a baking sheet. Bake until fish flakes easily (10 to 12 minutes).

4. Open packets and garnish with lime wedges before serving.

LEMON-LIME RICE

> 2 *cups water*
> ½ *teaspoon salt*
> 1 *cup white rice*
> 2 *tablespoons each lemon and lime juice*
> ½ *cup minced parsley (optional)*

1. Bring water, salt, and rice to a boil. Cover, reduce heat. Simmer until water is absorbed (20 minutes).

2. Mix in juice and parsley. Serve.

SPICY MEXICAN CORN

> 1 *package (10 oz) frozen corn*
> 2 *tablespoons water*
> 1 *can (4 oz) diced green chiles, drained*
> 1 *to 2 tablespoons hot salsa*
> 1 *jar (2 oz) pimientos, diced*

1. In a covered saucepan over low to medium heat, cook corn in the water until it begins to thaw (5 minutes).

2. Stir, add chiles, salsa, and pimientos; increase heat and cook until corn is tender (8 to 10 minutes).

CATCH OF THE DAY

Trout With Almonds

Sautéed Vegetable Medley

Wine suggestion:
Gewürztraminer
or Chenin Blanc

Fresh trout is at its best when prepared simply. Here, the fish are sautéed quickly, then served with a quick sauce of butter, lemon juice, and parsley, and garnished with toasted almonds. Complete the menu with the Sautéed Vegetable Medley and a loaf of crusty French bread.

COOKING PLAN

1. Assemble all ingredients and cooking equipment.

2. Heat water for vegetables.

3. Wash and cut up potatoes, carrot, onions, and mushrooms. Add potatoes to water.

4. Warm platter for fish in 200° F oven.

5. Sauté trout.

6. Add carrots and onions to potatoes; sauté mushrooms.

7. Turn trout.

8. Drain vegetables; sauté with mushrooms.

9. Remove trout to platter and prepare sauce.

10. Add basil to vegetables.

To Serve *Toss vegetables, pour sauce over trout, and garnish.*

TROUT WITH ALMONDS

Golden sautéed almonds are a crisp, flavorful contrast to the delicate trout. You can use almost any small whole fish in this recipe.

>   4 medium trout, cleaned
>   Lemon juice
>   Freshly cracked black pepper
>   6 tablespoons butter
>   2 tablespoons oil
>   ½ cup sliced almonds
>   ¼ cup each *lemon juice or white wine and minced parley*
>   Lemon slices and dill sprigs *(for garnish)*

1. Rub trout with lemon juice and pepper.

2. Warm serving platter for fish in 200° F oven.

3. In a wide frying pan large enough to hold the 4 trout (use 2 pans if necessary), melt 2 tablespoons of the butter with the oil over medium-high heat. Add trout and sauté until lightly browned on one side. Turn when edges become opaque and curl slightly (3 to 5 minutes). The fish is done when it flakes at the touch of a fork at the thickest portion near the backbone. Remove fish to warm platter. Wipe out pan.

4. Melt the remaining ¼ cup butter in pan. Add almonds and sauté until golden.

5. Combine lemon juice and parsley and add to almonds. Swirl and pour sauce over trout. Garnish with lemon slices and sprigs of dill.

Trout With Lemon-Dill Sauce

Complete steps 1 through 3. Melt ¼ cup butter in pan. Add 2 shallots, minced, *or* 2 tablespoons chopped yellow onion and sauté briefly. Add ¼ cup dry sherry, finely grated rind of 1 lemon, and 4 sprigs fresh dill or fennel, minced (or 1 teaspoon dried). Swirl and pour over trout.

SAUTÉED VEGETABLE MEDLEY

>   ¾ pound small new potatoes, quartered
>   1 large carrot, cut in sticks
>   4 small white onions, peeled and halved
>   2 tablespoons butter
>   ½ pound (20 medium) mushrooms, halved
>   1 teaspoon dried basil
>   Grated Parmesan, Romano, or Sapsago cheese *(for garnish; optional)*

1. In a large saucepan in boiling salted water to cover, cook potatoes 5 minutes. Add carrot and onions and cook 5 minutes more.

2. Meanwhile, melt butter in a large skillet; add mushrooms and sauté.

3. Drain boiled vegetables, add to skillet, and sauté briefly with mushrooms.

4. Add basil; toss vegetables to mix. Garnish with cheese if desired.

SPRING SALMON FEAST

Broiled Salmon Steaks

Lemon Mayonnaise

Tomatoes au Gratin

Fresh Asparagus

Wine suggestion:
Sauvignon Blanc

Celebrate the opening of fishing season with a special dinner of Broiled Salmon Steaks, served on their own or topped with Lemon Mayonnaise. Tomatoes au Gratin nestle among the salmon steaks for the last 10 minutes of broiling. Asparagus is in peak season from April to June. Dinner rolls make a nice addition to the meal.

COOKING PLAN

1. *Assemble all ingredients and cooking equipment.*

2. *Preheat broiler.*

3. *Melt butter for salmon. Halve tomatoes and grate cheese. Clean asparagus.*

4. *Brush salmon with butter and season. Place under broiler. Heat water for asparagus.*

5. *Assemble tomatoes and place in broiler. Cook asparagus.*

6. *Prepare Lemon Mayonnaise.*

7. *Turn salmon.*

To Serve *Remove salmon and tomatoes from broiler and place tomatoes in hollows of salmon steaks. Top asparagus and salmon with Lemon Mayonnaise. Garnish salmon.*

BROILED SALMON STEAKS

  4 salmon steaks (¾ in. thick)
  ¼ *cup melted butter*
  1 teaspoon dried marjoram
     Salt and freshly ground pepper
     Minced parsley (for garnish)

1. Preheat broiler. Brush salmon steaks well with butter on both sides. Sprinkle both sides of fish with marjoram and season to taste.

2. On oiled rack 4 inches from heat source, broil steaks until first side is lightly browned (5 to 8 minutes). Baste with butter, turn, baste again, and broil 5 to 8 minutes longer or until fish flakes easily at the touch of a fork. Garnish with parsley.

LEMON MAYONNAISE

  ⅔ *cup mayonnaise (at room temperature)*
     Juice of 1 lemon
  1 teaspoon Worcestershire sauce
     Salt and freshly ground pepper

Combine mayonnaise, lemon juice, Worcestershire sauce, and salt and pepper to taste.

TOMATOES AU GRATIN

  2 large tomatoes, halved or fluted
  2 tablespoons melted butter
  ½ *cup freshly grated Parmesan or Romano cheese*
  ¼ *cup bread or cracker crumbs*
  ½ *teaspoon each paprika and dried basil*
  2 tablespoons dry white wine, tomato juice, or chicken broth

1. Gently squeeze tomato halves to remove seeds.

2. Combine butter, cheese, crumbs, paprika, basil, and wine and divide evenly among tomato halves, pressing lightly into tomatoes.

3. Broil on oiled foil with salmon during last 10 minutes.

FRESH ASPARAGUS

  1½ to 2 pounds asparagus

1. Wash asparagus and cut or snap off tough ends.

2. In a large skillet in a little boiling salted water, lay spears parallel to one another, not more than 3 layers deep. Cook, uncovered, over high heat until stems are just tender when pierced with a fork (6 to 8 minutes).

Menu

FRIDAY NIGHT SEAFOOD DINNER

Scallops in Wine Sauce
Squash and Mushrooms With Herbs

Wine suggestion:
Pouilly-Fumé

Reward yourself at the end of the week with Scallops in Wine Sauce. To reduce the cost, substitute bite-sized chunks of fish for some of the scallops. A squash-and-mushroom side dish and sliced French bread make fitting accompaniments.

COOKING PLAN

1. *Assemble all ingredients and cooking equipment.*

2. *Cut up, chop, and grate ingredients for all dishes.*

3. *Preheat broiler.*

4. *Bring broth to a boil; add scallops.*

5. *Cook squash and mushrooms.*

6. *Make sauce for scallops and assemble dish.*

7. *Place scallops in broiler.*

To Serve *Remove scallops from broiler; garnish. Serve squash.*

SCALLOPS IN WINE SAUCE

> ¼ cup chicken or clam broth
> ¼ cup white wine
> ¼ cup finely chopped green onion or 2 shallots, minced
> ½ teaspoon dried tarragon
> 1 to 1½ pounds scallops, cut in halves
> 2 tablespoons each *butter and flour*
> ¼ cup freshly grated Parmesan cheese
> Lemon wheels (*for garnish*)

1. Preheat broiler. In a large skillet over high heat, bring broth, wine, onion, and tarragon to a boil.

2. Reduce heat to a simmer, add scallops, cover, and cook until scallops become opaque (5 minutes). Remove to ovenproof serving dish, reserving liquid.

3. In a small saucepan over medium heat, melt butter. Stir in flour, and cook until bubbly. Add reserved fish broth and cook until sauce thickens.

4. Pour sauce over scallops, sprinkle with Parmesan cheese. Place under broiler until lightly browned (2 to 3 minutes). Garnish with lemon.

Scallops Meunière In a large frying pan, melt ¼ cup butter. Add scallops and sauté until opaque. Add ¼ cup *each* lemon juice and parsley.

Scallops Amandine In a large frying pan, melt ¼ cup butter. Add scallops and sauté. In separate pan, melt 2 tablespoons butter. Add ¼ cup sliced or slivered almonds; sauté until golden. Add ¼ cup white wine or Marsala and 1 to 2 tablespoons Cognac or brandy. Pour over scallops.

SQUASH AND MUSHROOMS WITH HERBS

> 1 pound (4 small) crookneck or zucchini squash
> ½ pound (20 medium) mushrooms
> ¼ cup chicken broth
> ½ teaspoon dried basil
> Salt and freshly ground pepper

1. Trim ends of squash and quarter. Halve mushrooms.

2. Place in a large skillet with broth, basil, and salt and pepper to taste; cover; simmer until tender-crisp (6 to 8 minutes).

27

LOW-CALORIE SCALLOP DINNER

*Shrimp and Scallops in
Wine-Cheese Sauce*

Herbed Rice and Peas

*Wine suggestion:
Pinot Noir Blanc*

Even those who aren't on a diet will appreciate this light, flavorful dinner, prepared with a minimum of calories. Bake the shrimp, scallops, and sherried sauce in scallop-shell dishes for a charming presentation.

COOKING PLAN

1. *Assemble all ingredients and cooking equipment.*

2. *Preheat oven to 450° F; heat water in bottom of double boiler.*

3. *Remove peas from package to thaw slightly. Begin rice.*

4. *Cut up scallops, slice mushrooms, and grate cheese; measure other ingredients for seafood. Mince parsley for rice.*

5. *In double boiler, prepare sauce for seafood.*

6. *Sauté mushrooms. Poach scallops. Add shrimp.*

7. *Add parsley and peas to rice.*

8. *Combine seafood, mushrooms, and sauce; spoon into dishes. Add topping and place in oven.*

To Serve *Remove scallops from oven; garnish. Toss rice to mix ingredients, and serve.*

SHRIMP AND SCALLOPS IN WINE-CHEESE SAUCE

> 3 cups nonfat dry milk
> 2 tablespoons cornstarch
> 1 teaspoon salt
> ½ teaspoon *fines herbes* (or *pinch* each *parsley, chives, tarragon,* and *chervil*)
> 2 cups hot water
> ¼ cup safflower oil
> 1 cup shredded Monterey jack cheese
> 1 teaspoon butter (more if necessary)
> ½ pound (20 medium) mushrooms, sliced
> ¼ cup each *vermouth* and *dry sherry*
> ½ pound scallops, cut in halves
> ½ pound fresh or frozen small cleaned shrimp
> ¼ cup bread crumbs
> Minced parsley (for garnish)

1. Preheat oven to 450° F, and heat some water in bottom of a double boiler.

2. In top of double boiler, combine milk, cornstarch, salt, and herbs. Blend in water and oil.

3. Cook over rapidly boiling water, stirring often. When mixture thickens and begins to bubble, stir in half the cheese.

4. Meanwhile, in a frying pan, melt butter. Add mushrooms and sauté until barely tender. Remove mushrooms from pan.

5. Add vermouth and sherry to frying pan. Bring to a boil, reduce heat, and add scallops. Cook over medium-low heat until opaque (3 to 4 minutes). Add shrimp during last minute to heat through.

6. Fold scallops, shrimp, cooking liquid, and mushrooms into sauce in double boiler.

7. Spoon mixture evenly into 4 oven-proof dishes (scallop shells are nice). Sprinkle with remaining ½ cup cheese and the bread crumbs.

8. Bake, uncovered, at 450° F until sauce bubbles (5 to 8 minutes). Garnish with parsley.

HERBED RICE AND PEAS

> 1½ cups water
> ½ cup white wine or *an additional ½ cup water*
> 2 teaspoons lemon juice
> ½ teaspoon salt
> 1 teaspoon each *dried basil* and *thyme*
> 1 cup white rice
> 3 tablespoons minced parsley
> 1 package (10 oz) frozen petite peas

1. Bring water, wine (if used), lemon juice, salt, basil, thyme, and rice to a boil, cover, reduce heat, and simmer 15 minutes.

2. Quickly add parsley and peas (do *not* stir into rice), cover, and cook until all liquid is absorbed and peas are hot (about 5 minutes).

3. Mix peas and parsley into rice before serving.

CANDLELIGHT DINNER

Halibut With Almond Butter

*Fresh Broccoli Purée in
Fluted Tomato Halves*

*Wine suggestion:
German Riesling*

---

*Worcestershire-flavored
almond butter adds zest to
the mild taste of broiled
halibut, while a garnish of
sautéed almonds gives it
crunchy contrast. For the
side dish, a simple purée of
steamed broccoli and ricotta
cheese turns a fluted tomato
into edible art. Fresh rolls or
bread complete the menu.*

COOKING PLAN

1. *Assemble all ingredients and
cooking equipment.*

2. *Heat water for broccoli and melt
butter for almonds.*

3. *Mince parsley for almond butter
and garnish. Wash and chop broccoli; add to steamer.*

4. *Preheat broiler.*

5. *Toast almonds and flute
tomatoes.*

6. *Prepare almond butter, remove
from blender or food processor, and
chill. (It's not necessary to wash
container before puréeing broccoli.)*

7. *Broil halibut.*

8. *Purée broccoli. Turn halibut.*

To Serve *Fill tomatoes with purée;
serve remainder underneath. Dot
halibut with almond butter, and
garnish.*

HALIBUT WITH ALMOND BUTTER

- ½ cup unsalted butter
- 1 package (3½ oz) sliced or slivered almonds
- 2 to 3 tablespoons lemon juice
  Dash Worcestershire sauce
- 2 tablespoons minced parsley
- 4 halibut steaks or fillets (about 1½ lbs fish)
  Parsley sprigs (for garnish)

1. Preheat broiler. In a small frying
pan over medium heat, melt ¼ cup of
the butter until foamy and light
brown. (Cut the remainder in 4
pieces and set aside.) Add almonds
and sauté until lightly toasted. Place
all but a few almonds in blender or
food processor. Add lemon juice,
Worcestershire sauce, remaining butter, and half the minced parsley.
Blend or process 10 seconds. Remove
from container and chill.

2. Broil halibut 4 inches from heat
until first side is lightly browned (3 to
5 minutes). Turn and broil until fish
flakes easily at the touch of a fork (3
to 5 minutes more).

3. Dollop 2 tablespoons almond butter on each steak. Sprinkle with
reserved almonds and minced parsley. Garnish with parsley sprigs.

FRESH BROCCOLI PURÉE IN FLUTED TOMATO HALVES

- 1 bunch broccoli (2 lbs), coarsely chopped
- 2 large tomatoes, halved
- ½ to ¾ cup ricotta cheese, plain yogurt, or sour cream
- 1 tablespoon lemon juice
  Dash nutmeg, salt, and freshly ground pepper

1. Over boiling water, steam broccoli
until tender (10 to 15 minutes).

2. Gently squeeze tomato halves to
remove seeds. Set aside.

3. In a blender or food processor,
purée broccoli with ricotta. Season to
taste with lemon juice and spices. Fill
each tomato half with purée and
serve on a bed of purée.

31

CHICKEN FOR COMPANY

Chicken With Mushrooms

Fresh-Herb Pasta

Glazed Carrots

Wine suggestion:
Fumé Blanc or
Sauvignon Blanc

Guests will be impressed with this bit of kitchen showmanship. Be sure to try the sauce variations as well. On the side, serve baby carrots coated with a sweet, buttery glaze, and pasta tossed with fresh herbs.

COOKING PLAN

1. *Assemble all ingredients and cooking equipment.*

2. *Pound breasts.*

3. *Mince and slice ingredients for chicken. Mince herb for pasta. Scrub carrots.*

4. *Heat water for pasta.*

5. *Begin cooking carrots.*

6. *Sauté chicken.*

7. *Add pasta to boiling water.*

8. *Turn chicken.*

9. *Drain carrots and prepare glaze. Ignite chicken.*

To Serve *Drain pasta and toss with herb. Pour sauce over chicken, and serve carrots.*

CHICKEN WITH MUSHROOMS

> 8 boned chicken breast halves
> 1 tablespoon each butter and oil
> 2 cloves garlic, minced or pressed
> 3 or 4 green onions, sliced
> 1 cup sliced fresh mushrooms
> ⅓ cup Madeira wine

1. Pound breasts to a thickness of ¼ inch.

2. In a wide frying pan over medium-high heat, melt butter with oil. Pour half the fat into a second frying pan. Add breasts, skin side down. Add garlic, onions, and mushrooms to one of the pans. Sauté contents of both pans until chicken is lightly browned (3 to 5 minutes per side) and vegetables are tender.

3. Add Madeira to pan with vegetables, shaking pan to distribute. Heat and ignite. Serve chicken breasts with sauce poured over. (If necessary, chicken and sauce can be covered and kept warm in a 200° F oven until served.)

Chicken Amandine Complete steps 1 and 2, omitting vegetables. In a separate small frying pan, melt 1 tablespoon butter. Add 1 clove garlic, minced, and ½ cup sliced almonds; sauté until golden. Add ¼ cup Marsala, port, or dry sherry; swirl; and ignite. Pour sauce over chicken.

Chicken Rosemary Complete steps 1 and 2, substituting 1½ teaspoons minced fresh *or* ¼ teaspoon dried rosemary leaves, crumbled, for the onions and mushrooms. Omit step 3.

Chicken Véronique Complete steps 1 and 2, omitting vegetables. Keep chicken in 200° F oven to keep warm. Add ⅓ cup *each* lemon juice or dry white wine and whipping cream to frying pan. Bring to a boil and cook until slightly thickened. Stir in 1 cup grapes. Pour sauce over chicken.

Lemon Chicken Complete steps 1 and 2, omitting vegetables. Meanwhile, in a small saucepan melt 2 tablespoons butter. Add 2 tablespoons flour; 2 or 3 cloves garlic, minced; and 1 tablespoon grated lemon or orange rind (or 1½ teaspoons *each*). Cook over medium-high heat until bubbly. Stir in ½ cup dry white wine and cook until thickened. Pour sauce over chicken and garnish with minced parsley and lemon wheels.

FRESH-HERB PASTA

> 2 quarts water
> 1 teaspoon salt
> 8 ounces wide or medium noodles
> 1 tablespoon oil
> 1 tablespoon butter
>   Freshly ground pepper
> 2 tablespoons chopped fresh rosemary, thyme, or chives

1. In a large pot bring the water and salt to a boil.

2. Add noodles and oil and cook, uncovered, until pasta is al dente (5 to 8 minutes). Drain.

3. Toss with butter, pepper, and herb before serving.

GLAZED CARROTS

> 16 baby carrots, scrubbed and trimmed
> ¼ cup butter
> 2 tablespoons brandy or lemon juice
> 1 tablespoon brown sugar or honey

1. In a large skillet bring salted water to a boil. Add carrots, cover, and simmer until tender-crisp (10 to 15 minutes). Do not overcook. Drain.

2. Push carrots to one side and add butter, brandy, and sugar, stirring to combine. Sauté carrots over medium-high heat, shaking skillet, until carrots are well coated and lightly browned.

SUNDAY SPECIAL

Breast of Chicken à la Reimann

Savory Rice Pilaf

Broccoli Sauté

Wine suggestion:
Verdicchio

Want to stretch out the weekend? Cook an elegant, easy Sunday dinner. Breast of Chicken à la Reimann features toasted slivered almonds and a rich, creamy sauce flavored with Cognac. A simple rice pilaf and Broccoli Sauté round out the meal.

COOKING PLAN

1. *Assemble all ingredients and cooking equipment.*

2. *Chop onion and start rice.*

3. *Wash and chop broccoli; mince garlic. Chop shallots and slice chicken. Mince parsley for rice.*

4. *Sauté chicken and toast almonds.*

5. *Heat water and add broccoli.*

6. *Add sauce ingredients to chicken.*

7. *Heat Cognac and add to chicken.*

8. *Drain broccoli and sauté.*

9. *Add egg and cream to chicken.*

To Serve *Add parsley to rice and fluff. Fold almonds into chicken. Serve broccoli.*

BREAST OF CHICKEN À LA REIMANN

>   3   *whole chicken breasts, skinned and boned*
>   5   *tablespoons butter*
>   ¼   *cup chopped shallots or green onion*
>   ½   *cup slivered almonds*
>   2   *tablespoons flour*
>   ½   *cup white wine or chicken broth*
>   1   *tablespoon minced fresh or 1 teaspoon dried tarragon*
>   *Salt and freshly ground pepper*
>   ¼   *cup Cognac or brandy*
>   1   *egg yolk*
>   ⅓   *cup half-and-half*

1. Cut chicken breasts into ½-inch strips.

2. In a large frying pan over medium-high heat, melt 3 tablespoons of the butter. Add chicken and shallots and sauté just until chicken turns white. (Strips should be pink in centers.) Remove chicken and shallots from pan.

3. Meanwhile, in a small frying pan, melt remaining butter. Add almonds and sauté until golden.

4. Add flour to drippings in large frying pan and cook, stirring, until bubbly. Stir in wine and tarragon. Return chicken and shallots to pan and heat 2 to 3 minutes. Season to taste.

5. Add Cognac to pan, heat, and ignite.

6. Beat yolk lightly with half-and-half. Stir gradually into sauce and cook until sauce thickens. (Don't allow sauce to boil after adding yolk or it may curdle.)

7. Fold in almonds.

SAVORY RICE PILAF

>   2   *tablespoons butter*
>   ⅓   *to ½ cup chopped red onion*
>   1   *cup rice*
>   2   *cups chicken broth or water*
>   2   *tablespoons minced parsley*

1. In a saucepan melt butter. Add onion and sauté until soft and translucent.

2. Add rice; shake pan to coat rice well with butter.

3. Add broth, bring to a boil, cover, reduce heat, and simmer until liquid is absorbed (20 minutes).

4. A few minutes before rice is done, stir in parsley.

Note Optional additions to this pilaf include half a bay leaf and ¼ teaspoon paprika added with the broth; ¼ cup sliced fresh mushrooms, celery, pimiento, or almonds added 5 minutes before rice is done. Or substitute minced cilantro or watercress for the parsley.

BROCCOLI SAUTÉ

>   1   *bunch broccoli (2 lbs)*
>   2   *tablespoons butter*
>   1   *or 2 cloves garlic, minced*
>   1   *teaspoon lemon juice*

1. Wash and chop broccoli, including part of the stalks.

2. In a covered saucepan in boiling salted water to cover, cook broccoli until tender-crisp (8 to 10 minutes). Drain and set aside.

3. Melt butter in same saucepan; add garlic, lemon juice, and broccoli and quickly sauté until heated through.

DINNER FOR A RAINY NIGHT

Parmesan Chicken Breasts Sauté

Sautéed Peppers and Mushrooms

Braised Celery With Walnuts

Wine suggestion:
Frascati

Here's a dinner for a dreary evening that will leave you with time later to curl up with a good book and listen to the rain. Slice the vegetables for Braised Celery With Walnuts and Sautéed Peppers and Mushrooms while the breasts sauté. A last-minute garnish of fruit adds visual appeal.

COOKING PLAN

1. *Assemble all ingredients and cooking equipment.*

2. *Preheat oven to 200° F.*

3. *Pound breasts. Prepare coating mixtures. Dredge breasts and sauté 4 of them.*

4. *Wash and cut up peppers; mince garlic; clean and quarter mushrooms. Wash and slice celery, chop onion and walnuts, and grate lemon rind.*

5. *Melt butter. Sauté peppers and garlic.*

6. *Keep cooked breasts warm in oven; sauté second 4.*

7. *Heat water for celery; blanch.*

8. *Sauté mushrooms.*

9. *Sauté flavorings for celery and prepare garnish for chicken.*

To Serve *Toss celery with flavorings. Garnish chicken and serve peppers.*

PARMESAN CHICKEN BREASTS SAUTÉ

> 8 boned and skinned chicken breast halves
> ½ cup flour
> 1 egg, lightly beaten with 2 tablespoons water
> ¼ cup each *seasoned bread crumbs and Parmesan cheese, mixed*
> 2 tablespoons each *butter and oil*
>   Sliced avocado and citrus fruit (for garnish)

1. Pound breasts to a thickness of ¼ inch.

2. Place flour, egg, and crumb-cheese mixture in individual shallow dishes. In that order, dredge chicken pieces in each; place on a large platter.

3. Preheat oven to 200° F. In a wide frying pan, heat butter and oil. Add half the breasts and sauté until golden (3 to 5 minutes per side). Do not crowd pan. Keep cooked breasts warm in oven while sautéing remainder. Add more butter as needed.

4. Garnish as desired.

SAUTÉED PEPPERS AND MUSHROOMS

> 1 tablespoon butter
> 1 each *medium red and green pepper, julienned*
> 2 cloves garlic, minced
> 8 medium mushrooms, quartered

1. In frying pan over medium-high heat, melt butter. Add peppers and garlic; sauté until softened (8 to 10 minutes).

2. Add mushrooms and sauté until softened and tender (3 to 5 minutes). Serve on warmed platter.

BRAISED CELERY WITH WALNUTS

> 1 head celery, separated into stalks and washed
> 2 tablespoons butter
> 1 small onion, finely chopped
> ⅓ cup walnuts, coarsely chopped
>   Grated rind of 1 lemon

1. Cut celery diagonally into 1½-inch pieces. In a medium saucepan bring enough salted water to cover celery to a boil; add celery; blanch 5 minutes. Drain.

2. Meanwhile, in a large frying pan, melt butter. Add onion and walnuts and sauté briefly. Add lemon rind and celery. Toss to coat celery.

HARVEST SUPPER

Chicken Rosemary

Baked Squash Slices

Greek Salad

*Wine suggestion:
Orvieto or White Zinfandel*

A lot of good things from your garden can go into this supper: fresh rosemary for the chicken; lettuce, green onions, cucumbers, and cherry tomatoes for the Greek Salad; acorn squash and zucchini squash for Baked Squash Slices. Browning the chicken thighs on top of the stove, then baking them at high heat allows them to cook quickly. For a slightly unusual accompaniment, serve bran muffins warmed in a 450° F oven for 5 minutes.

COOKING PLAN

1. *Assemble all ingredients and cooking equipment.*

2. *Preheat oven to 450° F.*

3. *Sauté chicken.*

4. *Clean and slice squash and place in baking dish.*

5. *Add sauce ingredients to chicken; place chicken and squash in oven.*

6. *Prepare salad and dressing.*

To Serve *Toss salad with dressing. Remove squash and chicken from oven; garnish chicken.*

CHICKEN ROSEMARY

To vary the flavor of this dish, substitute basil, oregano, or thyme for the rosemary.

> ¼ cup olive oil
> 8 chicken thighs
>   Juice of half a lemon
> 1 tablespoon chopped fresh or 1 teaspoon dried rosemary, crumbled
>   Salt and freshly ground pepper
>   Lemon wheels and rosemary sprigs (for garnish)

1. Preheat oven to 450° F.

2. In ovenproof casserole or frying pan over medium-high heat, heat a little of the oil. Add chicken, skin side down, and sauté until golden (5 minutes).

3. Mix remaining oil with lemon juice, rosemary, and salt and pepper to taste. Turn chicken and pour sauce over it. Cover and bake until tender (15 to 20 minutes).

4. Garnish with lemon wheels and rosemary sprigs.

BAKED SQUASH SLICES

> 1 small acorn squash
> 1 large zucchini squash
>   Olive oil
>   Salt and freshly ground pepper

1. Wash both squashes. Halve acorn squash and remove seeds; peel. Cut zucchini in half lengthwise. Cut both squashes into ¼-inch slices and arrange in shallow baking dish.

2. Drizzle oil over squash and season to taste. Cover and bake in 450° F oven with chicken until tender (15 to 20 minutes).

GREEK SALAD

1 head red leaf or romaine
  lettuce
2 green onions, chopped, or
  1 red onion, sliced
1 small cucumber, peeled in
  alternate strips, quartered
  lengthwise, and sliced
3 ounces feta cheese, crumbled
8 Greek olives
¼ cup olive oil
3 tablespoons red wine vinegar
  Dash dry mustard
  Cherry tomatoes (optional)

1. Wash and dry greens; chop or tear in bite-sized pieces.

2. Add onions, cucumber, cheese, and olives and toss gently to combine.

3. Whisk together oil, vinegar, and mustard. Pour over salad and toss.

4. Garnish with cherry tomatoes if desired.

Menu

A TASTE OF MEXICO

Chicken Enchiladas

Avocado-Lettuce Salad

Beverage suggestion:
Sangría, margaritas, or
Mexican beer

This Mexican dinner is both quick to make and easy on the budget. Chicken Enchiladas are a good way to use leftover cooked chicken. For a heftier meal, add refried beans (heat one 16-ounce can in a small saucepan) topped with shredded Monterey jack cheese and chopped green onions. Provide a bowl of hot salsa or chopped jalapeño peppers for those who like their Mexican food fiery hot.

COOKING PLAN

1. Assemble all ingredients and cooking equipment.

2. Chop onion; shred chicken and cheese for enchiladas.

3. Preheat oven to 450° F.

4. Prepare enchilada filling.

5. Warm tortillas and assemble enchiladas. Place in oven.

6. Prepare salad and chop garnishes.

To Serve *Place garnishes—radishes, ripe olives, cilantro or parsley, sliced tomato, and peppers—in small bowls on table with salad and enchiladas. For a fuller meal, serve refried beans as a side dish.*

CHICKEN ENCHILADAS

1 tablespoon butter
⅓ cup chopped onion
2 cups cooked, shredded chicken
1 can (8 oz) stewed tomatoes
½ cup hot or mild salsa
1 can (4 oz) diced green chiles,
  drained (optional)
¼ to ½ teaspoon chili powder
  (or to taste)
  Salt and freshly ground
  pepper
1 can (11 oz) enchilada sauce
8 flour or corn tortillas
⅓ cup sour cream
¾ cup shredded Monterey jack or
  Cheddar cheese
  Chopped green onions (for
  garnish)

1. Preheat oven to 450° F. In a large frying pan, melt butter. Add onion and sauté until softened. Add chicken, tomatoes, ¼ cup of the salsa, the chiles (if used), chili powder, and salt and pepper to taste. Heat through. Keep warm over low heat.

2. Cover the bottom of an 8- by 12- by 2-inch baking pan with half the enchilada sauce.

3. One at a time, dampen each tortilla with water and heat on both sides in a hot, ungreased frying pan until soft and pliable.

4. Place ¼ cup of the chicken mixture on each tortilla and roll; place in baking dish. Top with remaining enchilada sauce, remaining salsa, the sour cream, and cheese.

5. Cover and bake until heated through (15 minutes). Serve garnished with green onions.

AVOCADO-LETTUCE SALAD

Half a head lettuce
1 avocado
½ cup sliced ripe olives
  Salsa or salad dressing

Tear lettuce in bite-sized pieces. Peel, pit, and slice avocado. Toss ingredients. Serve with salsa or dressing.

FLAVORS OF THE MIDDLE EAST

Moroccan Turkey Sauté

Couscous

*Mediterranean Green Bean
Salad With Tomatoes*

*Wine suggestion:
Chenin Blanc*

The spices of Moroccan cuisine enliven a sauté of cubed turkey and vegetables. Serve small bowls of grated coconut, toasted almonds, raisins, and chutney as condiments. Couscous, a grain dish made from semolina, is a traditional accompaniment.

COOKING PLAN

1. *Assemble all ingredients and cooking equipment.*

2. *Heat water for steaming; clean beans. (Trim ends 3 or 4 at a time for speed.) Place beans in steamer.*

3. *Cut up turkey and chop onion, garlic, and mushrooms.*

4. *Begin turkey sauté.*

5. *Mix dressing for beans.*

6. *Add remaining ingredients to turkey.*

7. *Heat broth for couscous.*

8. *Slice tomatoes and place condiments in bowls.*

9. *Add couscous to broth; remove from heat.*

10. *Assemble bean salad.*

To Serve *Fluff couscous. Accompany turkey and salad with small bowls of grated coconut, toasted almonds, raisins, chutney, and lemon wedges.*

MOROCCAN TURKEY SAUTÉ

  2 tablespoons olive oil
  1 turkey breast (1 to 1½ lbs), cut into 1-inch pieces
  *½ cup chopped green onion
     Half a red or green pepper, seeded and sliced (optional)*
  2 cloves garlic, minced or pressed
  ½ pound (20 medium) mushrooms, sliced
  1 cup chicken broth
  ½ cup raisins
  1 to 2 tablespoons brown sugar or honey
  1 teaspoon each cinnamon, allspice, and salt
  *1½ teaspoons ground cumin
     Mint (for garnish)*

1. In a large frying pan, heat oil. Add turkey, onion, pepper (if used), garlic, and mushrooms. Sauté over high heat 8 to 10 minutes.

2. Add broth, raisins, sugar, and spices and heat through (about 8 minutes). Serve alongside couscous, garnished with mint.

COUSCOUS

  3 cups chicken broth
  2 cups quick-cooking couscous

1. Bring broth to a boil and add couscous.

2. Immediately remove from heat, cover, and let stand 5 minutes. Fluff with a fork before serving.

MEDITERRANEAN GREEN BEAN SALAD WITH TOMATOES

  1 pound green beans, trimmed
  1 cup plain yogurt
  1½ teaspoons ground cumin
  2 large tomatoes, sliced

1. Over boiling water steam beans until tender-crisp (10 to 12 minutes). Place in freezer to cool quickly. Toss occasionally to cool evenly.

2. Meanwhile, in a small bowl mix yogurt and cumin.

3. To serve, mound beans in center of platter and surround with a ring of tomatoes. Top with dressing.

menu

ASIAN CHICKEN DINNER

Korean Chicken Thighs
Butter-Steamed Leeks
Sautéed Snow Peas
Beverage suggestion:
Sake

A mixture of soy sauce, sugar, garlic, vinegar, and hot pepper flakes forms the sauce for Korean Chicken Thighs. The rice and mild-flavored accompaniments set off the spicy taste of the chicken. Serve this meal with warm Japanese rice wine. Special sake carafes and cups are sold at stores featuring Asian items.

COOKING PLAN

1. *Assemble all ingredients and cooking equipment.*

2. *Start rice.*

3. *Preheat oven to 450° F.*

4. *Sauté chicken. Meanwhile, mince garlic and prepare sauce.*

5. *Put chicken in oven.*

6. *Clean leeks and grate cheese. Wash peas and mince garlic.*

7. *Cook leeks.*

8. *Remove cover from chicken and sauté snow peas.*

To Serve *Remove chicken from oven; fluff rice. Top leeks with cheese and serve peas.*

KOREAN CHICKEN THIGHS

  1 package (6 oz) wild-and-white rice
  2 tablespoons each butter and oil
  8 chicken thighs
  1 cup soy sauce
  ¼ cup sugar
  2 or 3 cloves garlic, minced or pressed
  ¼ cup red wine vinegar or white vinegar
1½ teaspoons crushed red pepper flakes

1. Preheat oven to 450° F.

2. Cook rice according to package directions (about 25 minutes).

3. In a large ovenproof skillet or casserole over medium-high heat, melt butter with oil. Add chicken and sauté, skin side down, until golden (5 minutes). Drain fat.

4. While chicken is cooking, mix soy sauce, sugar, garlic, vinegar, and red pepper flakes for sauce.

5. Turn chicken over, pour sauce over it, cover, and place in oven. Bake until tender (15 to 20 minutes), removing cover during last 5 minutes to crisp skin.

6. Serve with rice.

Mustard-Sauce Chicken Complete steps 1 through 3. Mix together 3 tablespoons Dijon mustard and 2 tablespoons red wine vinegar. Spread over chicken after turning and bake as directed in step 5.

Hawaiian Chicken Complete steps 1 through 3. Drain 1 can (8 oz) pineapple chunks, reserving ⅔ cup juice, *or* cut half a fresh pineapple into chunks. Distribute pineapple over chicken after turning; top with 2 limes or 1 lemon, thinly sliced, and 1 cup sliced almonds. Pour juice over canned pineapple (fresh pineapple needs no juice) and bake as directed in step 5.

Indian Chicken Complete steps 1 through 3, adding 1 small red onion, chopped, with chicken. Mix together 1 cup plain yogurt; ¼ cup tomato paste; 1 or 2 cloves garlic, minced; 2 teaspoons curry powder; ½ teaspoon ground coriander; ¼ teaspoon *each* ground cumin and ginger; and salt and pepper to taste. Spread over chicken after turning and bake as directed in step 5.

BUTTER-STEAMED LEEKS

1 bunch leeks (about 3)
2 tablespoons butter
¼ cup water
Freshly grated Parmesan cheese (for garnish)

1. Trim root ends of leeks and remove most of green leaves. Split lengthwise and wash under cold water, separating leaves to clean thoroughly.

2. In a large skillet over medium-high heat, melt butter until it browns slightly.

3. Add leeks and the water, cover, and increase heat to high. Cook until tender (3 to 5 minutes). Sprinkle with cheese before serving.

SAUTÉED SNOW PEAS

1 pound fresh snow peas
1 tablespoon butter
1 or 2 cloves garlic, minced or pressed
Salt and freshly ground pepper

1. Wash and drain snow peas; remove ends if desired.

2. In a large frying pan over medium-high heat, melt butter; add garlic and sauté briefly. Add snow peas and sauté until shiny and heated through (2 to 3 minutes). Season to taste.

SUMMER TOSTADA SUPPER

Mexican Ground Turkey Pita
Lettuce-and-Cilantro Salad
Beverage suggestion:
Mexican beer with lime wedges

A quick, light supper of spiced ground turkey, served tostada style atop a warm pita and cold shredded lettuce, is just the thing for a balmy summer night. A salad of lettuce tossed with cilantro, jicama, and a piquant salsa dressing echoes the Mexican theme.

COOKING PLAN

1. Assemble all ingredients and cooking equipment.
2. Preheat oven to 350° F.
3. Chop all turkey dish ingredients.
4. Cook turkey.
5. Warm pita bread in oven.
6. Prepare salad and dressing.

To Serve *Dress salad. Remove bread from oven and assemble turkey pitas.*

MEXICAN GROUND TURKEY PITA

1 tablespoon butter
1 pound ground turkey
½ cup chopped red onion
3 to 4 tablespoons salsa
1 teaspoon dried oregano
⅛ teaspoon ground cumin
½ teaspoon salt
¼ teaspoon freshly ground pepper
4 whole pita breads, warmed (see Note)
2 cups shredded iceberg lettuce
1 avocado, sliced
¼ cup sour cream or plain yogurt
Additional salsa
2 medium tomatoes, cut in wedges
8 ripe olives

1. In a large frying pan over high heat, melt butter. Add turkey, breaking up with a fork.

2. Add onion, salsa, and spices and cook until turkey is golden and juices are clear.

3. To assemble each serving: place a whole pita on each plate. Top with a quarter of the lettuce, turkey mixture, avocado, sour cream, and salsa. Garnish with tomato and olives.

Note To warm pitas, wrap in a damp towel and heat in a 350° F oven for 10 to 15 minutes.

LETTUCE-AND-CILANTRO SALAD

1 head each *butter and red leaf lettuce, torn in bite-sized pieces*
Half a jicama or daikon, coarsely shredded or sliced
1 bunch cilantro, stems removed
½ cup taco sauce or salsa
¼ cup salad oil
3 tablespoons vinegar

1. Mix lettuce, jicama, and cilantro.

2. Thoroughly combine taco sauce, oil, and vinegar and pour over salad. Toss and serve.

TURKEY TONIGHT

Turkey Breast Cutlets

Steamed Kale and Pearl Onions

Parsleyed Parsnips

Wine suggestion:
Sylvaner Riesling
or Fumé Blanc

Turkey cutlets are an excellent low-cost meat, adaptable to almost any veal recipe. Asparagus-and-Cheese Cutlets, pictured at left, is only one way to cook this many-splendored meat. Try all the variations given here. Poppy seed rolls make a nice accompaniment to the cutlet dinners.

COOKING PLAN

1. *Assemble all ingredients and cooking equipment.*

2. *Pound cutlets.*

3. *Clean parsnips; mince parsley. Clean kale, peel onions, and slice lemon.*

4. *Heat water for parsnips and for kale. Begin cooking parsnips.*

5. *Place egg-milk mixture and flour in 2 bowls and coat cutlets.*

6. *Warm platter for turkey in 250° F oven.*

7. *Sauté cutlets and begin cooking kale.*

8. *Make sauce for cutlets.*

9. *Add flavorings to parsnips.*

To Serve *Pour sauce over cutlets; garnish. Serve kale and parsnips.*

TURKEY BREAST CUTLETS

Turkey has a mild flavor that lends itself to numerous taste combinations. Treated like veal, it's an excellent substitute at an affordable price. You can also use pounded turkey tenderloin in this recipe.

    1 to 1½ pounds turkey breast
      cutlets or 1 turkey breast
      (1½ to 2 lbs), sliced
      into cutlets
    1 egg lightly beaten with
      ¼ cup milk
    1 cup flour
    6 tablespoons butter
    2 tablespoons oil
    ¼ cup lemon juice
      Minced chives or parsley
      (for garnish)

1. Pound cutlets between 2 sheets of plastic wrap (do not tear meat) to a thickness of ⅛ inch.

2. Dip cutlets in egg-milk mixture, then in flour. Shake off excess. To brown correctly, cutlets should be coated just before cooking.

3. Warm serving platter in 250° F oven.

4. In a large frying pan over medium-high heat, melt 2 tablespoons of the butter with the oil. Divide fat between 2 large frying pans and add coated cutlets. Sauté until golden (3 minutes per side). Transfer to warm platter.

5. Add lemon juice and remaining ¼ cup butter to one of the frying pans, bring to a boil, and reduce slightly. Pour sauce over cutlets and sprinkle with chives.

Cutlets Saltimbocca Complete steps 1 through 4. Top each cutlet with 1 slice prosciutto and 1 slice provolone cheese. Broil until cheese melts and turns golden.

Cutlets Piccata Complete steps 1 through 4. Add ¼ cup *each* lemon juice, butter, and minced parsley to one frying pan. Mix in 2 tablespoons capers, heat, and pour over cutlets.

Cutlets Marsala Complete steps 1 through 4. Add ¼ cup butter; 2 or 3 cloves garlic, minced; and ¼ cup chopped mushrooms to a frying pan. Brown mushrooms, add ⅓ cup Marsala wine and ¼ cup minced parsley. Heat. Pour over cutlets.

Asparagus-and-Cheese Cutlets Complete steps 1 through 4. Top each cutlet with 2 or 3 cooked asparagus spears and 1 slice *or* 2 tablespoons grated Swiss cheese. Broil until cheese turns golden. Garnish with quartered lemon slices and minced parsley.

Mustard Cutlets Complete steps 1 through 4. Pour ¼ cup white wine into a frying pan, bring to a boil, and reduce by half. Stir in ⅔ to 1 cup whipping cream and 3 to 4 tablespoons Dijon mustard. Reduce over high heat until thickened. Pour over cutlets.

Peppery Turkey Tarragon Complete steps 1 through 4. Pour ½ cup white wine into one frying pan, bring to a boil, and reduce. Add 1 to 2 tablespoons chopped fresh tarragon leaves *or* 1 teaspoon dried, 2 to 3 tablespoons drained green peppercorns, and ⅔ cup whipping cream. Reduce over high heat until thickened. Pour over cutlets.

Turkey Parmigiana Preheat oven to 450° F. Complete steps 1 through 4. Place a layer of cutlets in a large baking dish, top with ½ cup *each* tomato sauce and shredded mozzarella or provolone cheese. Add remaining cutlets, overlapping slightly, and an additional ½ cup each tomato sauce and shredded cheese. Bake until bubbly (5 to 10 minutes).

Turkey With Mushrooms Complete steps 1 through 4. Pour ½ cup sherry into a frying pan. Add 1 tablespoon butter, 2 to 3 tablespoons Dijon mustard, and 1½ to 2 cups sliced fresh mushrooms. Cook over high heat until mushrooms are tender and liquid is reduced by half. Stir in ⅔ to 1 cup whipping cream and reduce over high heat until thickened. Pour over cutlets.

Turkey Sorrel (or Spinach)
Complete steps 1 through 4. In a frying pan melt 3 tablespoons butter. Add ¼ cup chopped onion (optional) and 1 bunch chopped fresh sorrel or spinach leaves. Sauté until wilted (3 to 4 minutes). Remove. Add ¼ cup white wine; bring to a boil to reduce. Stir in 1 cup whipping cream and the sorrel. Salt and pepper to taste. Serve over cutlets.

STEAMED KALE AND PEARL ONIONS

¼ pound pearl onions, peeled
1 bunch kale, coarsely chopped
   Lemon wedges (for garnish)

Place onions and then kale in steamer over boiling water and cook until kale is wilted (8 to 10 minutes). Garnish with lemon wedges.

PARSLEYED PARSNIPS

1½ pounds (8 to 10 medium) parsnips, peeled and trimmed
2 tablespoons butter
½ teaspoon dried basil
¼ cup minced parsley

In a large, covered skillet, cook parsnips in boiling water to cover until tender-crisp (about 15 minutes). Drain. Add butter, basil, and parsley. Toss to coat parsnips.

A TASTE OF NORMANDY

Veal Normande
Rice With Almonds
Tomato-Cucumber Salad
With Herb Dressing

Wine suggestion:
Gamay Beaujolais

Apples and dairy products are plentiful in the French province of Normandy. Veal Normande features a sauce of Calvados, sliced apples, and sour cream. The salad takes advantage of summer's bounty of vine-ripened tomatoes and cucumbers.

COOKING PLAN

1. Assemble all ingredients and cooking equipment.

2. Start rice.

3. Wash and slice vegetables for salad; assemble. Make dressing.

4. Mince parsley and slice apples for veal; measure other ingredients.

5. Pound and coat veal.

6. Preheat oven to 200° F and sauté veal.

7. While veal cooks, sauté almonds for rice.

8. Remove veal and prepare sauce.

To Serve *Mix rice and almonds; serve salads. Top veal with a bit of the sauce, and serve remainder separately. Garnish veal. Pour dressing over salads.*

VEAL NORMANDE

Boneless chicken breasts or turkey breast slices, pounded to a thickness of ⅛ inch, may be substituted for the more expensive veal.

1½ pounds boneless veal slices (¼ in. thick)
½ cup flour
1 tablespoon each *butter and oil*
¼ cup Calvados (apple brandy), brandy, or dry white wine
2 tart green apples, cored and thinly sliced
½ cup sour cream
   Minced parsley (for garnish)

1. Place veal between 2 pieces of plastic wrap and pound to a thickness of ⅛ inch. Coat with flour.

2. Warm serving platter in 200° F oven. Melt butter with oil in a wide frying pan over medium heat.

3. Add veal and sauté until lightly browned but still pale pink inside (about 2 minutes per side). Remove to warm platter.

4. Add Calvados, scraping bottom of pan to free browned bits. Add apple slices and sauté 3 to 5 minutes. Reduce heat, stir in sour cream, and simmer until warm.

5. Serve veal topped with apple slices and sauce, and garnished with parsley.

Veal Marsala Complete steps 1 through 3. To frying pan add 2 tablespoons flour. Cook, stirring, until bubbly. Stir in ½ cup Marsala wine; cook until thickened. Pour sauce over veal and garnish with minced chives.

Veal Amandine Complete steps 1 through 3. To frying pan, add 1 tablespoon butter; 1 clove garlic, minced; and ½ cup sliced almonds. Sauté until golden. Add ¼ cup Marsala, port, or dry sherry. Bring to a boil and ignite. For a creamy sauce, stir in ¼ cup sour or whipping cream. Pour sauce over veal and garnish with lemon wheels.

RICE WITH ALMONDS

- 2 cups water
- ½ teaspoon salt
- 1 cup white rice
- 1½ tablespoons butter
- 1 bag (2½ oz) sliced almonds

1. Bring water, salt, and rice to a boil. Cover, reduce heat, and simmer until all water is absorbed (20 minutes).

2. In a small frying pan, melt butter. When it froths, add almonds and sauté until lightly browned.

3. Stir nuts and butter into rice before serving.

TOMATO-CUCUMBER SALAD WITH HERB DRESSING

For an attractive presentation, take a few minutes to arrange each salad individually. Include slices of avocado, radish, turnip, or jicama if you wish. Serve at room temperature for fullest flavor.

- 4 medium tomatoes, sliced
  Half a cucumber, peeled in alternate strips and thinly sliced
- 1 small red or yellow onion, thinly sliced and separated into rings
  Watercress sprigs
  (for garnish)

Herb Dressing

- ¼ cup olive or salad oil
- 2 tablespoons lemon juice
- 1 teaspoon Dijon mustard
- 1 teaspoon each minced fresh or ¼ teaspoon dried tarragon and thyme

1. Arrange tomato and cucumber in a ring, alternating slices. Top with onion rings. Garnish center with watercress sprigs.

2. Pour Herb Dressing over salads.

Herb Dressing Thoroughly combine oil, lemon juice, mustard, tarragon, and thyme.

VEAL FOR A PARTY

Veal With Champagne Sauce
Minted Green Peas With Lettuce
Wine suggestion:
Brut or extra dry Champagne

Celebrate a birthday or anniversary with this impressive main dish. The tang of the minted vegetables plays off well against the rich, creamy sauce. Add crusty rolls and, of course, chilled Champagne.

COOKING PLAN

1. *Assemble all ingredients and cooking equipment.*

2. *Remove peas from package to thaw slightly.*

3. *Prepare mushrooms, chop shallots, and slice lemon for veal.*

4. *Shred lettuce and mince parsley for peas.*

5. *Warm platter in 200° F oven.*

6. *Pound, slice, and coat veal. Sauté.*

7. *Begin cooking peas.*

8. *Remove veal from pan and prepare sauce.*

9. *While sauce cooks, add lettuce to peas.*

To Serve *Pour sauce over veal and garnish. Season peas and serve.*

VEAL WITH CHAMPAGNE SAUCE

A thick, rich sauce of cream, Champagne, and mushroom caps enhances this elegant entrée. Use veal scallops or ask your butcher to cut a boneless veal roast into ¼-inch-thick slices across the grain.

- 1½ pounds boneless veal slices (¼ in. thick)
- ½ cup flour
- ¼ teaspoon salt
- ⅛ teaspoon freshly ground pepper
- ⅛ teaspoon ground nutmeg
- 2 tablespoons each butter and oil
- ½ pound (20 medium) mushrooms, stems removed
- 2 shallots, chopped, or 2 tablespoons minced onion
- ¼ cup Champagne (see Note)
- ½ cup each whipping cream and sour cream
  Chopped green onion and lemon wheels (for garnish)

1. Place veal slices between 2 sheets of plastic wrap and pound to a thickness of ⅛ inch. Cut into strips across the grain.

2. Place flour, salt, pepper, and nutmeg in a paper bag. Add veal and shake to coat.

3. Warm serving platter in oven.

4. In a wide frying pan over medium-high heat, melt butter with oil

5. Add half the veal and sauté, tossing occasionally, until strips turn a light golden brown (3 to 5 minutes). Remove to heated platter.

6. Sauté remaining veal strips. Keep warm in oven on platter.

7. Add mushroom caps and shallots to pan and sauté briefly, scraping pan to release browned bits.

8. Return any veal juices from platter to pan. Add Champagne and whipping cream and reduce liquid by half over high heat.

9. Lower heat to simmer and stir in sour cream. Heat through.

10. To serve, spoon sauce over veal. Sprinkle with onions. Surround with lemon wheels.

Note One-fourth cup dry white wine can be substituted for Champagne.

Veal Parmesan Prepare broiler. Prepare veal as directed in step 1. Coat veal with a mixture of ¼ cup *each* flour and freshly grated Parmesan cheese, ¼ teaspoon salt, ⅛ teaspoon pepper, and ¼ teaspoon paprika. Sauté in 1 tablespoon *each* butter and oil as directed in steps 5 and 6;

remove to ovenproof serving dish. Top with ½ cup shredded mozzarella cheese and a dash of paprika. Broil until cheese is golden and bubbly (2 to 3 minutes). Sprinkle with minced parsley and garnish with lemon wheels.

MINTED GREEN PEAS WITH LETTUCE

> *2 tablespoons butter*
> *1 package (10 oz) frozen peas*
> *2 cups (packed) shredded lettuce*
> *1 tablespoon chopped fresh or*
> *1 teaspoon dried mint leaves,*
> *   crushed*

> *2 tablespoons minced parsley*
> *   (optional)*
> *   Salt and sugar (optional)*
> *   Mint sprigs (for garnish)*

1. In a large skillet over medium heat, melt butter. Add peas (breaking up with a fork), cover, and cook until thawed (about 5 minutes).

2. Add lettuce, chopped mint, and parsley (if used) and cook, uncovered, until lettuce wilts. Toss occasionally. Season to taste and garnish with mint.

Menu

CLASSIC FILET MIGNON DINNER

*Beef Filet With Béarnaise
and Tomato*

Fruited Savoy Cabbage

*Wine suggestion:
Cabernet Sauvignon*

*Béarnaise sauce, a variation
of hollandaise sauce
flavored with tarragon, is a
classic accompaniment for
red meat. This blender
version is quick and easy to
prepare. If you wish, you
can cook the steaks outdoors
on the grill, but you'll need
to allow additional time to
ready the coals for cooking.
A good-quality baguette will
enhance the meal.*

COOKING PLAN

1. *Assemble all ingredients and
cooking equipment.*

2. *Preheat broiler.*

3. *Wash and slice cabbage, apples,
and tomatoes.*

4. *Place steaks in broiler.*

5. *Prepare béarnaise.*

6. *Sauté cabbage.*

7. *Turn steaks.*

8. *Add apples to cabbage.*

9. *Remove steaks from broiler.*

To Serve *Garnish steaks with tomato and béarnaise. Accompany with
cabbage.*

BEEF FILET WITH BÉARNAISE AND TOMATO

Filet mignon is the cut traditionally used in this recipe, but less expensive cuts such as flank, top round, and chuck can be substituted. Reduce cooking time on these cuts to 4 to 6 minutes per side for rare meat. The 30-minute cooking plan assumes the steaks will be cooked indoors in the broiler. If you choose to grill the steaks outdoors over coals, allow additional time to ready the coals for cooking.

> 4 *filet mignon steaks
> (1½ to 2 in. thick)*
> 2 *large tomatoes*

Blender Béarnaise

> ¼ *cup each white wine vinegar
> and vermouth or white wine*
> 1 *teaspoon dried tarragon*
> ¼ *cup minced shallots*
> 1 *cup butter*
> 3 *egg yolks*

1. Preheat broiler.

2. Slice tomatoes and set aside.

3. About 20 minutes before serving, place steaks in broiler 4 inches from heat source. Broil 7 or 8 minutes per side for rare meat.

4. To serve, top each steak with 1 or 2 slices of tomato and cover with Blender Béarnaise.

Blender Béarnaise In a small saucepan bring vinegar, vermouth, tarragon, and shallots to a boil. Reduce to 3 tablespoons. In a separate saucepan melt butter. In a blender whirl yolks just until blended. Add reduced wine mixture and blend briefly. Add butter, a droplet at a time at first, blending continuously on high speed. As mixture thickens, increase butter to a thin stream. Keep sauce warm by placing blender container in a pan of lukewarm water if desired.

Note If sauce "breaks," or curdles, beat in 1 tablespoon water.

FRUITED SAVOY CABBAGE

- 2 tablespoons butter
- 1 medium Savoy cabbage, trimmed and cut crosswise into ½-inch strips
- 1 cup thinly sliced green apple
- 2 tablespoons honey
- 1 teaspoon salt

1. In a large frying pan over medium-high heat, melt butter. Add cabbage. Sauté for 4 minutes. Toss often.

2. Stir in apple, honey, and salt. Sauté, tossing occasionally, until tender-crisp (4 to 6 minutes).

51

SPRING STEAK-AND-ASPARAGUS DINNER

*Steak With Peppercorn
Cream Sauce*

White Rice

Asparagus With Lemon Butter

*Wine suggestion:
Australian Shiraz or Cabernet
Sauvignon*

---

*Green peppercorns are the
unripe berries of the pepper
vine, and are usually sold
canned. Teamed with Dijon
mustard, they add a
delightful pungency to the
creamy sauce served here
atop thinly sliced sautéed
steak. Add fresh buttered
asparagus and you have a
springtime celebration.*

COOKING PLAN

*1. Assemble all ingredients and
cooking equipment.*

2. Start rice.

*3. Chop onion and wash watercress
for steak. Clean asparagus.*

4. Brown steak.

*5. Heat water for asparagus. Begin
to cook it when you turn the steak.*

6. Add brandy to steak.

*7. Make sauce for steak and slice
meat.*

*8. Make lemon butter for
asparagus.*

To Serve *Fluff rice. Spoon sauce
over meat and garnish. Serve
asparagus.*

STEAK WITH PEPPERCORN CREAM SAUCE

- *1 teaspoon each butter and oil*
- *1 top round, sirloin, or
flank steak (1½ lbs)*
- *¼ cup brandy*
- *¼ cup minced shallots or
½ cup minced red onion*
- *2 to 3 tablespoons green
peppercorns, rinsed*
- *⅓ cup each dry white wine and
whipping cream*
- *1 tablespoon Dijon mustard*
- *1 tablespoon minced fresh or
½ teaspoon dried tarragon
Salt and freshly ground
pepper
Watercress sprigs
(for garnish)*

1. In a wide frying pan over medium-high heat, melt butter with oil. Add steak and brown well on both sides (3 to 5 minutes per side).

2. Add brandy to pan, heat, and ignite, shaking until flames die. Remove meat to a carving board.

3. Add to pan shallots, peppercorns, wine, whipping cream, mustard, tarragon, and salt and pepper to taste. Increase heat to high, and reduce sauce until shiny bubbles form.

4. While sauce cooks, slice meat diagonally (across the grain for flank steak). Stir meat juices into sauce.

5. To serve, top steak with sauce and garnish with watercress.

Steak With Mushroom-and-Wine Sauce
Cook steak as directed in step 1; remove to carving board. In frying pan melt 1 tablespoon butter. Add ¼ pound mushrooms, sliced, and 2 cloves garlic, minced; sauté briefly. Combine ⅓ cup *each* red wine or port and beef broth with a mixture of 1 tablespoon cornstarch, 1 teaspoon Dijon mustard, ½ teaspoon anchovy paste (optional), and 2 tablespoons minced parsley or green onion. Add to pan, bring sauce to a boil, reduce heat, and simmer until thickened. Pour over sliced steak.

Steak Provençale
Cook steak as directed in step 1; remove to carving board. In frying pan heat 1 tablespoon oil. Add 1 red or green pepper, sliced; 1 small red onion, thinly sliced; 1 large tomato, peeled, seeded, and cut in 8 wedges; and 2 cloves garlic, minced. Sauté until vegetables are tender. Add ¼ cup beef broth; ½ teaspoon dried oregano; ⅛ teaspoon dried rosemary, crumbled; and 1 tablespoon chopped fresh basil or parsley. Stir to combine and pour over sliced steak.

WHITE RICE

- *2 cups water*
- *½ teaspoon salt*
- *1 cup white rice
Minced parsley (for garnish)*

Bring water, salt, and rice to a boil. Cover, reduce heat, and simmer until all water is absorbed (20 minutes). Garnish with parsley.

ASPARAGUS WITH LEMON BUTTER

- *1½ to 2 pounds asparagus*
- *2 tablespoons butter
Juice of half a lemon*
- *⅛ teaspoon nutmeg*

1. Wash asparagus and cut or snap off tough ends.

2. In a wide frying pan in a little boiling water, lay spears parallel to one another, not more than 3 layers deep. Cook, uncovered, over high heat until stems are just tender when pierced with a fork (6 to 8 minutes). Drain and set aside.

3. Melt butter in frying pan; stir in lemon juice and nutmeg. Pour over asparagus and toss to coat.

Asparagus Orientale
Complete steps 1 and 2. Substitute 1 tablespoon soy sauce, 2 tablespoons sesame seed, and 2 teaspoons grated fresh ginger root for the lemon-flavored butter.

STEAK, QUICK AND EASY

Steak Bonne Femme

Steamed New Potatoes

Glazed Sesame-Seed Carrots

*Wine suggestion:
Gamay or burgundy*

For a relaxed evening get-together, serve Steak Bonne Femme, a classic dish of sautéed sirloin steak topped with onions and mushrooms. Potatoes are always a great companion for steak, and Glazed Sesame-Seed Carrots, with their hint of orange, add a touch of the unusual.

COOKING PLAN

1. *Assemble all ingredients and cooking equipment.*

2. *Heat water in steamer.*

3. *Wash and slice potatoes and carrots.*

4. *Slice onion and mushrooms; mince garlic and parsley; grate orange rind.*

5. *Place potatoes and carrots in steamer, with potatoes on bottom.*

6. *Warm platter in 200° F oven.*

7. *Sauté vegetables for steaks.*

8. *Toast sesame seed.*

9. *Sauté steaks.*

10. *Glaze carrots.*

To Serve *Sprinkle potatoes with parsley. Spoon sauce over steak and serve carrots.*

STEAK BONNE FEMME

1 tablespoon each *butter and oil*
1 large *red onion, thinly sliced and separated into rings*
½ pound (20 medium) *mushrooms, sliced*
1 clove *garlic, minced*
1½ pounds *top sirloin steak (¾ in. thick), cut in 4 equal pieces*
¼ cup *beef broth
Salt and freshly ground pepper*

1. Warm serving platter in 200° F oven.

2. In a large frying pan over medium heat, melt butter with oil. Add onion, mushrooms, and garlic and sauté until softened.

3. Increase heat to brown onion and reduce juices from mushrooms. Remove vegetables from pan.

4. In same pan over high heat, adding a little more butter and oil if necessary, brown steaks until done to taste (3 to 4 minutes per side for rare). Remove to heated platter.

5. Add broth to pan; bring to a boil to reduce liquid, scraping pan to loosen browned bits.

6. Reduce heat, stir in reserved onion-mushroom-garlic mixture, and heat through. Season to taste. Spoon sauce over steaks.

STEAMED NEW POTATOES

10 to 12 small *thin-skinned red or white potatoes
Minced parsley (for garnish)*

1. Scrub potatoes, but do not peel. Slice thinly.

2. Place in basket or perforated container over boiling water. Place carrots on top. (Carrots for Glazed Sesame-Seed Carrots go on top.) Steam until tender (about 15 minutes).

3. Garnish with parsley.

GLAZED SESAME-SEED CARROTS

8 to 10 medium *carrots, peeled and cut in 3-inch sticks*
7 teaspoons *butter*
2 tablespoons *sesame seed*
1 tablespoon *honey*
1 tablespoon *grated orange rind*
1 teaspoon *grated fresh ginger root (optional)*

1. Place carrots in steamer above potatoes. (See recipe for Steamed New Potatoes.) Cook until tender (about 15 minutes).

2. While carrots steam, melt 1 teaspoon of the butter in a medium frying pan and toast sesame seed until golden.

3. When carrots are tender, add remaining butter, the honey, orange rind, and ginger (if used) to the pan. Remove carrots from steamer, add to pan, and toss to glaze.

MEXICAN DINNER
ON THE PATIO

Beef Burritos

Corn on the Cob
With Cumin Butter

Sliced Melon With Lemon

Beverage suggestion:
Sangría or Mexican beer

Burritos are great fast food:
The tortilla-wrapped
packages of spicy ground
beef and grated cheese go
together quickly and almost
make a meal in themselves.
Continue the Mexican theme
with corn on the cob spread
with cumin-spiced butter,
and offer Sliced Melon With
Lemon as a cooling finish
to the meal.

COOKING PLAN

1. *Assemble all ingredients and cooking equipment.*

2. *Chop and grate all ingredients for burritos, including toppings. Cut up limes and lemons.*

3. *Prepare burrito filling.*

4. *Heat water for corn.*

5. *Mix cumin-flavored butter.*

6. *Slice melon.*

7. *Warm tortillas in 350° F oven.*

8. *Add corn to boiling water.*

9. *Assemble burritos.*

To Serve *Place toppings and melon on table. Serve burritos, and corn with cumin-flavored butter.*

BEEF BURRITOS

Burritos are simply warmed tortillas filled with beans, meat, or a mixture of the two. After filling, they may be eaten as is, baked in a 450° F oven briefly, or barbecued over coals.

    1 pound ground beef
    1 medium onion, chopped
    1 can (16 oz) refried beans
    1 can (8 oz) stewed tomatoes
    ⅓ cup hot or mild salsa
    1 cup sliced ripe olives
       Canned or fresh diced
       green chiles
       Sliced jalapeño chiles
       (optional)
    1 teaspoon each chili powder
       and salt
    4 large (10- or 12-in.) flour
       tortillas, warmed
       (see Note)
    1 cup shredded Cheddar or
       Monterey jack cheese
       Optional garnishes: salsa,
       avocado slices, cherry
       tomatoes, and hot chiles

1. In a large frying pan, sauté ground beef and onion until meat is browned and onion is soft.

2. Stir in refried beans, stewed tomatoes, salsa, olives, chiles, chili powder, and salt. Heat until bubbly.

3. Place about ½ cup of filling down the center of each tortilla; top with a sprinkling of cheese. Fold top and bottom edges over filling, and then fold in sides.

4. Garnish as desired.

Note To warm tortillas, wrap in foil and place in 350° F oven for 10 minutes.

Chicken or Sausage Burritos In a medium frying pan, warm 1 to 1½ cups shredded cooked chicken or thinly sliced cooked sausage (chorizo or linguica) with 1 can (7 oz) diced green chiles and their juice. Down the center of each warmed tortilla, place ½ cup shredded Monterey jack cheese, one fourth of the chicken-chile mixture, 3 tomato slices, 3 red onion rings, 3 avocado slices, and 3 cilantro sprigs. If desired, heat briefly in 450° F oven or over coals.

CORN ON THE COB WITH
CUMIN BUTTER

    4 to 6 ears fresh corn, husked
    ½ cup butter, softened and
       mixed with 1 teaspoon cumin
    2 limes, cut in wedges

1. In a large pot bring to a boil enough water to cover corn generously.

2. Add ears one at a time. Cover pot and remove from heat at once. Allow corn to remain in hot water until tender (about 5 minutes).

3. Drain and serve with cumin-flavored butter and lime wedges (to squeeze over corn).

SLICED MELON WITH LEMON

    1 cantaloupe, honeydew, or
       Crenshaw melon
       Lemon wheels and mint sprigs
       (for garnish; optional)

1. Halve and seed melon. Cut into slices.

2. Garnish with lemon wheels and mint sprigs if desired.

EASY STROGANOFF SUPPER

Hamburger Stroganoff

Caraway Seed Noodles

Zesty Green Beans

*Wine suggestion:
Rosé of Cabernet*

This version of the classic beef dish uses inexpensive hamburger instead of steak. Golden egg noodles tossed with butter and caraway seed offer a perfect complement of texture and flavor. Choose a light red wine such as rosé of Cabernet to go with this meal.

COOKING PLAN

1. Assemble all ingredients and cooking equipment.

2. Mince and slice ingredients for Stroganoff. Shape meatballs.

3. Sauté meatballs. While they cook, prepare ingredients for beans.

4. Add butter, sliced mushrooms, onion, and garlic to meatballs.

5. Heat water for noodles.

6. Cook beans. Add noodles to boiling water.

7. Add sour cream to meatballs.

8. Add vinegar to beans.

To Serve *Drain noodles and toss with butter and seed. Garnish Stroganoff and serve beans.*

HAMBURGER STROGANOFF

This entrée is a real lifesaver if you're pressed for time. Garnishing with cilantro (fresh coriander leaves or Chinese parsley) gives the dish zest.

- 1 *pound ground beef*
- ⅓ *cup minced onion*
- 1 *stalk celery, minced*
- ½ *cup finely chopped fresh mushrooms*
- 3 *cloves garlic, minced*
- 2 *to 3 tablespoons minced parsley*
- ¼ *teaspoon Worcestershire sauce*
- 1 *tablespoon sherry (optional)*
- ½ *teaspoon each salt and pepper*
- 1 *tablespoon butter*
- ½ *pound (20 medium) mushrooms, sliced*
- 1 *pint (2 cups) sour cream or 1 cup each yogurt and sour cream*
  Chopped cilantro (for garnish; optional)

1. Mix together beef, ¼ cup of the minced onion, the celery, chopped mushrooms, two thirds of the garlic, the parsley, Worcestershire, sherry (if used), and salt and pepper. Shape into 1-inch-diameter balls.

2. In a large frying pan over medium-high heat, sauté meatballs 5 minutes. Drain fat.

3. Add butter, sliced mushrooms, remaining onion, and remaining garlic and sauté 5 minutes more.

4. Stir in sour cream, reduce heat, and simmer until sauce is heated through (5 minutes).

5. Garnish with cilantro if desired.

CARAWAY SEED NOODLES

- 2 *quarts water*
- 1 *teaspoon salt*
- 8 *ounces medium noodles*
- 1 *tablespoon oil*
- 2 *tablespoons butter*
- 1 *teaspoon caraway seed*

1. In a large pot bring the water and salt to a boil.

2. Add noodles and oil and cook, uncovered, until noodles are al dente (5 to 8 minutes). Drain.

3. Toss with butter and caraway seed before serving.

ZESTY GREEN BEANS

- 2 *tablespoons butter or oil*
- 1 *clove garlic, minced*
- 1 *pound green beans, cut diagonally in 1-inch lengths*
  Half a small red pepper, seeded and cut in ½-inch strips
- 5 *tablespoons water*
- 2 *teaspoons wine vinegar*

1. In a large skillet over medium-high heat, melt butter. Add garlic and sauté briefly. Add beans, pepper, and water; stir. Cover and steam until tender-crisp (about 6 minutes).

2. Remove cover, add vinegar, and increase heat to high to evaporate most of the liquid (1 to 2 minutes).

HAMBURGER EXTRAVAGANZA

*Classic Hamburgers With
International Toppings*

*Red-and-Green
Cabbage Salad*

*Beverage suggestion:
Beer*

*Here's a burger for every
taste, from an elegant
Russian Burger topped with
sour cream and caviar to a
sturdy Burger Ranchero
sandwiched with cheese, egg,
and olives. For the juiciest
and most flavorful burgers,
buy coarsely ground meat
with 20 percent fat, and use
about 5 ounces of meat for
each patty. Line your broiler
with aluminum foil to
simplify cleanup.*

COOKING PLAN

1. *Assemble all ingredients and
cooking equipment.*

2. *Choose your topping and fit it
into the Cooking Plan.*

3. *Wash and slice vegetables for
salad. Prepare and refrigerate.*

4. *Preheat broiler.*

5. *Shape burgers and broil. Allow a
total time of 8 minutes (for rare) to
16 minutes (for well done).*

6. *Turn burgers.*

7. *Place muffins under broiler.*

To Serve *Remove salad from
refrigerator. Assemble burgers.*

CLASSIC HAMBURGERS WITH INTERNATIONAL TOPPINGS

The main recipe features a cooked-with-the-burger topping, but you may substitute any of the variations, which should be added to plain broiled burgers immediately before serving. For a cookout or other special occasion, make a selection of toppings and offer diners a choice.

Sourdough French rolls, whole wheat pita bread, or cheese-flavored English muffins are alternatives to plain English muffins or the traditional hamburger bun.

> 1¼ pounds ground beef (20% fat)
> Salt and freshly ground
> pepper
> 1 sweet red onion, thinly sliced
> 1 large green pepper, seeded
> and cut in ¼-inch-thick rings
> 2 teaspoons dried oregano,
> crushed and mixed with 1 to
> 2 tablespoons olive oil
> 4 English muffins, split

1. Preheat broiler.

2. Season ground meat with salt and pepper and shape into 4 patties.

3. Place on lightly greased broiler rack and broil 4 inches from heat source until desired doneness is reached. Broiling time *per side* is:

Rare	4 minutes
Medium	6 minutes
Well done	7 to 8 minutes

4. After turning burgers, top each with 1 slice onion, 1 green pepper ring, and one fourth of the oregano-oil mixture.

5. During last 3 minutes of cooking time, place muffins, cut side up, on rack with burgers to brown.

Guacamole Burgers Complete steps 1 through 3. Combine 1 small avocado, mashed, (1 cup); 1 small tomato, chopped, *or* ¼ cup Mexican salsa; 1 tablespoon lemon juice; ½ teaspoon chili powder; and salt and pepper to taste. Place a spoonful on each broiled burger and top with sliced olives and chopped tomato.

French Tarragon-Butter Burgers Complete steps 1 through 3. In a small saucepan combine ½ to 1 teaspoon dried tarragon with 1 tablespoon white wine vinegar. Boil until liquid is almost gone; cool slightly. Mix tarragon and 3 tablespoons minced parsley into ¼ cup butter, softened. Top each broiled burger with one fourth of the butter.

Mushroom-and-Wine-Sauced Burgers Complete steps 1 through 3. In a medium frying pan, melt 1 tablespoon butter. Add ¼ pound mushrooms, sliced, and 2 cloves garlic, minced. Sauté briefly. Combine 1 tablespoon cornstarch, 1 teaspoon Dijon mustard, ½ teaspoon anchovy paste (optional), and 2 tablespoons minced parsley or green onion. Mix in ⅓ cup *each* dry red wine or port and beef broth. Add to mushrooms, bring to a boil, reduce heat, and simmer until thickened. Spoon over broiled burgers.

Carrot-Yogurt Burgers Complete steps 1 through 3. Combine 1 medium carrot, shredded; ¼ cup yogurt; and 2 tablespoons wheat germ. Place a spoonful on each broiled burger. Sprinkle with 1 teaspoon sunflower seed. Garnish with minced parsley.

Burgers Provençale Complete steps 1 through 3. In a medium frying pan, heat 1 tablespoon olive oil. Add half a red and half a green bell pepper, sliced; 1 medium red or yellow onion, chopped; and 2 cloves garlic, minced. Sauté until limp. Sprinkle with ½ teaspoon dried oregano; ⅛ teaspoon dried rosemary, crumbled; and 1 tablespoon chopped fresh basil or parsley. Stir to combine and spoon over broiled burgers.

Russian Burgers Complete steps 1 through 3. On each broiled burger place 1 tablespoon sour cream or yogurt. Top each with 2 teaspoons red, black, or golden caviar. Garnish with chopped green onion or chives.

Burgers Rancheros Complete steps 1 through 3. Substitute sliced French bread for the muffins. Top each bread slice with 2 slices of cheese and broil 1 minute. Add a slice of tomato, a broiled burger, a fried or poached egg, and sliced ripe olives or chopped chives for garnish. For more zest, add chopped chiles or salsa.

Open-Faced Anchovy Burgers Complete steps 1 through 3. Substitute 2 sourdough French rolls, halved, for the muffins. Top each roll half with 2 slices Swiss or Monterey jack cheese; broil until cheese melts. Sauté 1 cup sliced red onions and divide evenly among the roll halves. Top each with a broiled burger. Arrange anchovy fillets and pimiento slices in a checkerboard pattern on burgers. Place halved green olives in the "squares."

RED-AND-GREEN CABBAGE SALAD

Half a head green cabbage, sliced or shredded
Half a large red onion, thinly sliced or chopped
½ to ⅔ cup mayonnaise
Juice of half a lemon
¼ teaspoon lemon pepper or black pepper

Mix cabbage, onion, mayonnaise, lemon juice, and pepper; chill.

61

SPICY CHICKEN LIVER DINNER

Curried Chicken Livers

Elbow Macaroni

Butter-Steamed Chard

Beverage suggestion:
Beer or ale

This nutritious dinner is especially rich in iron. Chicken livers sautéed in a spicy mixture of mustard, curry powder, ginger, and garlic offer an intriguing combination of flavors. The two sauce variations provide other opportunities for serving chicken livers.

COOKING PLAN

1. *Assemble all ingredients and cooking equipment.*

2. *Wash and chop chard; slice lemons.*

3. *Halve livers; chop and measure other ingredients.*

4. *Start water for macaroni.*

5. *Sauté livers.*

6. *Add macaroni to boiling water.*

7. *Butter-steam chard stems.*

8. *Add peas to livers.*

9. *Add chard leaves to stems.*

To Serve *Drain macaroni and toss with butter, garnish liver, and serve chard with lemon wedges.*

CURRIED CHICKEN LIVERS

   1 pound chicken livers
   1 tablespoon each butter and oil
   1 tablespoon dry mustard
   2 to 3 tablespoons curry powder
   1 tablespoon ground ginger
   1 clove garlic, minced
   1 cup frozen peas

1. Rinse and drain livers; pat dry. Cut livers in halves.

2. In a heavy frying pan over medium-high heat, melt butter with oil. Add mustard, curry powder, ginger, and garlic and sauté 10 seconds.

3. Add livers and sauté until browned (8 to 10 minutes).

4. Add peas and cook, covered, until tender (about 5 minutes).

5. Serve over Elbow Macaroni.

Livers With Madeira Wine Sauce
Prepare livers as directed in step 1. In a medium frying pan, melt 2 tablespoons butter. Add ⅔ cup sliced fresh mushrooms; sauté briefly. Add 1 cup chicken broth and ⅓ cup Madeira. Stir in 2 teaspoons tomato paste. In a small bowl blend 2 teaspoons cornstarch with 1 tablespoon cold water. Stir into sauce and simmer 10 minutes. While sauce simmers, sauté livers in 1 tablespoon *each* butter and oil. Pour sauce over livers.

Livers With Creole Sauce Prepare livers as directed in step 1. In a saucepan heat 2 tablespoons olive oil. Add ½ cup *each* chopped red onion and celery. Cook, stirring, until onion becomes limp. Add 2 cups chopped fresh or canned plum tomatoes; 1 bay leaf; ½ teaspoon dried rosemary, crumbled; and ¼ to ½ teaspoon dried red pepper flakes. Bring to a boil, reduce heat, and simmer 10 minutes. While sauce simmers, sauté livers in 1 tablespoon *each* butter and oil. Pour sauce over livers.

ELBOW MACARONI

   2 quarts water
   1 teaspoon salt
   8 ounces elbow macaroni (try green and yellow vegetable pasta, for color)
   2 tablespoons olive oil
   1 teaspoon lemon juice
   1 tablespoon butter
   Minced parsley (for garnish)

1. In a large pot bring the water and salt to a boil.

2. Add macaroni, oil, and lemon juice and cook until pasta is al dente (6 to 9 minutes). Drain.

3. Toss with butter and garnish with parsley.

BUTTER-STEAMED CHARD

   1¼ to 1½ pounds fresh chard
   2 tablespoons butter
   2 tablespoons water
   Lemon wedges

1. Wash chard. Slice stems diagonally and chop leaves coarsely.

2. In a large, heavy skillet, melt butter. Add chard stems; cover and cook 3 to 4 minutes.

3. Add leaves and sprinkle with the water. Cover and cook until tender (3 to 4 minutes longer).

4. Serve with lemon wedges.

SAUTÉED SUPPER

Hearty Calves' Liver

Baked Potato Slices

Zucchini and Tomatoes Provençale

Wine suggestion:
Zinfandel

This menu features a wealth of hearty flavors—onions and liver, herbed potatoes, and vegetables sautéed with garlic and thyme. Be careful not to overcook the liver; properly cooked, calves' liver is tender and delicious.

COOKING PLAN

1. *Assemble all ingredients and cooking equipment.*

2. *Preheat oven to 400° F. Prepare potatoes and place in oven.*

3. *Slice mushrooms, onions, and zucchini. Mince chives, parsley, and garlic.*

4. *Check potatoes and turn if browned. Dredge liver.*

5. *Sauté mushrooms and onions for liver. Begin zucchini sauté.*

6. *Check potatoes; turn off oven if they are done.*

7. *Sauté liver. Add tomatoes to zucchini.*

To Serve *Remove potatoes from oven and garnish. Top liver with sauce and serve zucchini.*

HEARTY CALVES' LIVER

  1 pound thinly sliced
     calves' liver
  ½ *cup flour seasoned with ½*
     teaspoon salt and ⅛ teaspoon
     freshly ground pepper
  6 *tablespoons butter*
  ½ *cup each sliced onions*
     and fresh mushrooms
     Minced chives (for garnish)

1. Coat liver with seasoned flour.

2. In a large, heavy frying pan, melt 2 tablespoons of the butter. Add onions and mushrooms and sauté until tender. Remove from pan.

3. Add remaining butter to pan and heat until it foams. Without crowding, sauté liver 2 minutes per side over medium-high heat. Do *not* overcook.

4. Top with onions and mushrooms and sprinkle with chives.

Brandied Liver Prepare liver as directed in steps 1 through 3, omitting onions. Remove from pan. Add 2 to 3 tablespoons brandy to pan, scraping to release browned bits, and spoon sauce over sautéed liver.

BAKED POTATO SLICES

  4 *large potatoes*
     Salt and pepper
     Chopped parsley and butter

1. Preheat oven to 400° F. Scrub potatoes and cut crosswise into ⅛-inch-thick slices.

2. Arrange on oiled cookie sheet. Turn slices and season as they brown. Bake until tender (about 20 minutes). Garnish with parsley and butter.

ZUCCHINI AND TOMATOES PROVENÇALE

  2 *firm zucchini (about 1 lb)*
  2 *tablespoons olive oil*
  1 *clove garlic, minced*
 12 *cherry tomatoes*
  ½ *teaspoon dried thyme*
     Salt and pepper

1. Trim ends from zucchini and quarter lengthwise. Cut crosswise into ½-inch-thick slices.

2. In a large skillet over medium-high heat, heat oil. Add zucchini and garlic and sauté until zucchini begins to brown (5 minutes).

3. Add tomatoes and thyme and sauté until tomatoes are warm (2 to 4 minutes). Season to taste.

END-OF-SUMMER SUPPER

Savory Broiled Pork Chops
Bulgur Pilaf
Golden Cauliflower
Wine suggestion:
Pinot Noir

Broil or barbecue thick, juicy pork chops on one of the last evenings of summer, when the nights are getting longer and the evening air is crisp. The mustard coating on the chops makes a tart counterpoint to the cheesed cauliflower. Bulgur, or cracked wheat, is a grain popular in the Middle East.

COOKING PLAN

1. *Assemble all ingredients and cooking equipment.*

2. *Preheat broiler.*

3. *Spread chops with mustard, add thyme, and place in broiler.*

4. *Chop vegetables for pilaf and sauté with bulgur. Add broth and simmer.*

5. *Wash and slice cauliflower; shred cheese.*

6. *Check chops and turn if ready.*

7. *Cook cauliflower; a few minutes later, add cheese and paprika.*

8. *Test chops by piercing with a fork.*

To Serve *Add parsley, pimiento, and seasonings to pilaf. Remove chops from broiler. Serve cauliflower.*

SAVORY BROILED PORK CHOPS

> 3 tablespoons Dijon mustard
> 4 loin pork chops (¾ in. thick)
> 1 teaspoon dried thyme, crushed
> Salt and pepper

1. Preheat broiler. Spread half the mustard evenly over chops; sprinkle with half the thyme.

2. Broil 6 inches from heat source 10 to 12 minutes. Turn chops, spread with remaining mustard. Sprinkle with thyme, salt, and pepper to taste.

3. Broil second side until nicely browned (10 to 12 minutes). Juices should run clear when chop is pierced with a fork at thickest point.

BULGUR PILAF

> 2 tablespoons butter
> 1 to 3 cloves garlic, minced
> ¼ cup each *chopped yellow or green onion, mushrooms, and celery*
> 1 cup bulgur
> 2 cups chicken broth
> 2 to 3 tablespoons minced parsley
> 2 tablespoons chopped pimiento (optional)
> Salt and pepper

1. In a large skillet or saucepan over medium-high heat, melt butter. Add garlic, onion, mushrooms, celery, and bulgur and sauté, stirring occasionally, until bulgur is golden.

2. Add broth, bring to a boil, reduce heat, and simmer, covered, until liquid is absorbed (15 minutes).

3. Just before serving, stir in parsley, pimiento (if used), and salt and pepper to taste.

GOLDEN CAULIFLOWER

> 3 tablespoons butter
> 4 cups thinly sliced cauliflower
> ⅓ cup water
> 1 cup shredded Cheddar cheese
> 1 teaspoon paprika

1. In a large skillet melt butter. Add cauliflower and the water. Cover and steam over high heat for 3 minutes.

2. Top with cheese and paprika; cover and continue steaming until cheese melts and cauliflower is tender (about 2 minutes).

PORK CHOPS FOR A WINTER NIGHT

Apricot Pork Chops

Poppy Seed Egg Noodles

Sautéed Cabbage and Peas

Wine suggestion:
Rioja or Chianti Classico

This cheerful meal is perfect for the dead of winter—hot, homey, and filling. Apricot-sauced pork chops with a hint of port and ginger are delightful combined with Poppy Seed Egg Noodles and a simple sauté of slivered cabbage and peas.

COOKING PLAN

1. Assemble all ingredients and cooking equipment.

2. Brown chops.

3. Slice onion; sauté a few slices to garnish chops.

4. Add remaining ingredients to chops and simmer.

5. Heat water for noodles.

6. Wash and shred cabbage.

7. Add noodles to boiling water.

8. Sauté cabbage. Then add peas.

9. Drain noodles and warm butter or cream.

To Serve *Toss noodles with poppy seed and butter or cream. Garnish chops and serve cabbage.*

APRICOT PORK CHOPS

> 1 tablespoon butter
> 4 thin loin pork chops
> 1 cup sliced red or yellow onion
> ½ cup dried apricot halves
> 1 cup beef broth
> ½ cup port or red or white wine (or increase broth to 1½ cups)
> ¼ cup orange marmalade
> 1 teaspoon grated fresh ginger root or ½ teaspoon ground ginger
> 1 clove garlic, minced
>   Dash nutmeg
> 1 tablespoon cornstarch
>   Sautéed onion slices (for garnish)

1. In a large skillet over medium-high heat, melt butter. Add chops and brown 2 to 3 minutes per side.

2. Scatter onion and apricots over chops. Combine broth, port, marmalade, ginger, garlic, and nutmeg; pour over meat.

3. Bring to a boil, reduce heat, cover, and simmer until meat is tender (15 to 20 minutes).

4. Mix cornstarch with a tablespoon of the sauce and then add to skillet. Cook, stirring, until sauce thickens.

5. Garnish with sautéed onion slices.

Peachy Pork Chops Brown chops as directed in step 1 and remove from pan. Add ¼ cup *each* chopped onion and green pepper and sauté until tender. Return meat to pan and add 1 cup beef or chicken broth; 1½ teaspoons dried thyme; 1 teaspoon dry mustard; and 1 clove garlic, minced. Cover and simmer 15 minutes. Add 2 fresh peaches, halved, *or* 1 can (16 oz) peach halves, drained, and 4 green pepper rings; simmer 5 minutes more. To serve, top each chop with sauce, a heated peach half, and a pepper ring.

Sweet-and-Sour Pork Chops

Brown chops as directed in step 1. Add ¾ cup beef or chicken broth and 1 tablespoon each soy sauce, brown sugar, and vinegar and simmer 10 minutes. Add half a green pepper, sliced; 4 small white onions, quartered; and 1 can (8 oz) pineapple chunks, drained. Cook, covered, until vegetables are tender (10 minutes). Mix 1 tablespoon cornstarch with a little of the sauce and then add to pan. Cook, stirring, until sauce thickens.

POPPY SEED EGG NOODLES

> 2 quarts water
> 1 teaspoon salt
> 8 ounces thin or medium egg noodles
> 3 tablespoons butter, whipping cream, or sour cream
> 2 tablespoons poppy seed

1. In a large pot bring the water and salt to a boil.

2. Add noodles and cook, uncovered, until al dente (4 to 8 minutes, depending on size). Drain.

3. Warm butter or cream in pot in which noodles were cooked. Add noodles and poppy seed and toss gently to mix.

SAUTÉED CABBAGE AND PEAS

> 2 tablespoons butter
>   Half a small head cabbage, finely sliced or shredded (2½ cups)
> 1 package (10 oz) frozen petite peas
>   Nutmeg and freshly ground white pepper to taste

1. In large skillet melt butter. Add cabbage and sauté until slightly wilted (3 minutes).

2. Add peas and nutmeg and pepper to taste and cook, stirring, until heated through (3 to 5 minutes).

DINNER ON THE DOUBLE

Ham With Hot Peaches

Almond-Grape Slaw

Wine suggestion:
Pinot Noir Blanc

This menu, particularly quick to prepare, makes a good weeknight dinner. Try substituting fresh pears for the peaches, or vary the glaze as suggested for other quick, delicious ham dinners. The crunchy slaw features shredded cabbage tossed with sunflower seed, wheat germ, and grapes and a dressing lightened with yogurt. If you wish, you can add whole wheat rolls (warm in a 450° F oven for 5 minutes).

COOKING PLAN

1. *Assemble all ingredients and cooking equipment.*

2. *Preheat oven to 450° F.*

3. *Wash cabbage, cut apart to form bowl, and shred center. Wash grapes. Slice peaches for ham.*

4. *Combine ingredients for slaw and refrigerate.*

5. *Bread ham slices and brown.*

6. *Assemble ham dish and place in oven.*

7. *Spoon slaw into cabbage bowl.*

To Serve *Garnish slaw. Remove ham from oven and serve.*

HAM WITH HOT PEACHES

> 1 *egg*
> ½ *cup milk*
> 1 *pound sliced ham (about ¼ in. thick)*
> ¾ *to 1 cup bread crumbs*
> 2 *tablespoons each butter and oil*
> 4 *fresh peaches, sliced, or 1 can (16 oz) sliced peaches, drained*
> ¼ *cup honey*

1. Preheat oven to 450° F.

2. Beat together egg and milk. Coat each ham slice first with egg mixture and then with bread crumbs.

3. In a large frying pan, heat butter and oil. Add ham and brown slices on both sides.

4. Form slices into rolls and arrange in a row in a baking dish.

5. Place peach slices over ham and drizzle with honey. Bake until honey glazes (5 minutes).

Spicy Glazed Ham Combine ¼ cup *each* honey and soy sauce and 1 teaspoon Dijon or regular mustard. Spread glaze on one side of each ham slice (do not bread or roll) and broil, glazed side up, 5 to 6 inches from heat source until slices are heated through (3 to 4 minutes).

Ham With Lime-Mustard Glaze Mix ¼ cup dry mustard. Add 2 tablespoons *each* cold water, white wine vinegar, and lime juice. If glaze is too nippy, add a little olive oil and a pinch of sugar. Spread glaze on one side of each ham slice (do not bread or roll) and broil, glazed side up, 5 to 6 inches from heat source until slices are heated through (3 to 4 minutes).

Ham With Tarragon-Mustard Glaze Mix ¼ cup dry mustard. Add 1 to 2 tablespoons *each* cold water and tarragon wine vinegar, and ½ teaspoon dried tarragon. If glaze is too nippy, add a little olive oil and a pinch of sugar. Spread glaze on one side of each ham slice (do not bread or roll) and broil, glazed side up, 5 to 6 inches from heat source until slices are heated through (3 to 4 minutes).

Cranberry- or Chutney-Glazed Ham Spread about ⅓ cup cranberry relish or chutney on one side of each ham slice (do not bread or roll). Broil, glazed side up, 5 to 6 inches from heat source until slices are heated through (3 to 4 minutes).

ALMOND-GRAPE SLAW

> 1 *medium head (2½ lbs) green cabbage, with outer leaves*
> ¼ *cup each plain yogurt and mayonnaise*
> 1 *to 2 teaspoons honey*
> ½ *cup seedless red or green grapes*
> 1 *tablespoon lemon juice*
> ¼ *cup sunflower seed or slivered almonds*
> 2 *to 3 tablespoons wheat germ*
> ¼ *teaspoon each celery seed and salt*
> ⅛ *teaspoon freshly ground black or white pepper*
> *Sunflower seed or slivered almonds (for garnish; optional)*

1. Wash cabbage and turn back several rows of outer leaves. With a paring knife, cut stem at base of leaves to release center of cabbage, leaving outer leaves attached to stem to form a bowl. Drain outer leaves.

2. Shred center of cabbage, place in mixing bowl, and fold in yogurt, mayonnaise, honey, grapes, lemon juice, the ¼ cup sunflower seed, wheat germ, and seasonings. Chill.

3. Serve slaw in cabbage bowl. Sprinkle with additional sunflower seed if desired.

GERMAN WURST SUPPER

Bratwurst

Spaetzle

Red Cabbage With Apples

Beverage suggestion:
German beer

This supper features a traditional combination: bratwurst served with sautéed onion, red cabbage, and Spaetzle. To complete the German flavor of the meal, accompany it with a spicy German or Dijon mustard, rounds of pumpernickel, kosher dill pickles, and German beer.

COOKING PLAN

1. *Assemble all ingredients and cooking equipment.*

2. *Heat water for bratwurst and for spaetzle.*

3. *Chop apple, cabbage, and onion for red cabbage dish. Slice onion and green pepper and grate cheese for bratwurst.*

4. *Simmer sausages.*

5. *Add spaetzle to boiling water.*

6. *Sauté onion for bratwurst. Separately, sauté onion for cabbage dish.*

7. *Add liquid, and then apple and cabbage, to cabbage dish.*

8. *Remove spaetzle from heat and let stand.*

9. *Brown sausages and warm onions.*

To Serve *Arrange bratwurst on onions; garnish. Drain spaetzle, toss with butter, and garnish. Serve cabbage.*

BRATWURST

    4 *bratwurst*
    1 *tablespoon oil*
    1 *cup sliced red or yellow onion*
    ½ *cup grated Swiss cheese,*
       at room temperature
    4 *green pepper rings*
       (for garnish)
       German-style mustard
       Pumpernickel loaf
       Kosher dill pickle spears

1. In boiling water to cover, simmer sausages 10 minutes. Drain.

2. Meanwhile, in a large frying pan, heat oil. Add onion and sauté until golden and limp (5 to 7 minutes). Remove from pan and keep warm. Add drained sausages and sauté until golden. Add onions and warm briefly.

3. Place sausages on a bed of sautéed onion; top with cheese and garnish with green pepper.

4. Serve with a spicy German mustard, rounds of pumpernickel, and crisp kosher dill pickle spears.

SPAETZLE

Packaged dried spaetzle—noodle-like German egg dumplings—can be found in the imported food sections of many supermarkets, or at delicatessens or specialty food shops. If they aren't available, substitute curly egg noodles.

Follow directions on a 10-ounce package of spaetzle. Cook in boiling salted water (or beef or chicken broth, for more flavor) for 10 minutes. Then remove from heat and let stand in cooking water 10 minutes more. Drain and toss with butter. It's traditional to sprinkle spaetzle with bread crumbs before serving. Garnish with minced parsley.

RED CABBAGE WITH APPLES

    2 *tablespoons salad oil*
    1 *onion, coarsely chopped*
    ¼ *cup cider vinegar*
    2 *tablespoons brown sugar*
       or honey
       Salt and freshly ground
       pepper
    1 *green apple, cored and*
       thinly sliced
    1 *small head red cabbage,*
       coarsely shredded

1. In a large frying pan heat oil. Add onion and sauté until softened (5 minutes). Add vinegar, sugar, and salt and pepper to taste; stir to mix.

2. Add apple and cabbage. Bring liquid to a boil, reduce heat to medium, cover, and cook until cabbage wilts (10 minutes). Stir occasionally to coat cabbage with vinegar-sugar mixture.

DINNER-IN-A-POT

Kielbasa One-Pot Supper

Dark Rye With Melted Cheese

*Spinach Salad With
Lemon-Soy Dressing*

*Beverage suggestion:
Beer or ale*

For a hearty meal to serve by the fire on a winter night, try this easy one-pot dish of kielbasa cooked with potatoes, onion, broccoli, and carrots. Delicious Dark Rye With Melted Cheese holds its own against the flavorful kielbasa, and the fruited spinach salad is enhanced by a tangy Lemon-Soy Dressing.

COOKING PLAN

1. *Assemble all ingredients and cooking equipment.*

2. *Dice bacon and chop vegetables for one-pot dish.*

3. *Fry bacon. Cook vegetables.*

4. *Wash and chop spinach; slice other vegetables for salad. Make salad dressing.*

5. *Preheat broiler.*

6. *Add sausage and bacon to one-pot dish.*

7. *Toast bread; slice cheese; assemble salad.*

8. *Top bread with cheese and broil.*

To Serve *Place salad and dressing on table. Slice bread and serve with one-pot dish.*

KIELBASA ONE-POT SUPPER

> *4 to 6 slices bacon, diced*
> *1 tablespoon butter*
> *4 medium new potatoes, scrubbed and sliced (leave skins on)*
> *1 medium red onion, sliced*
> *1 bunch broccoli, stems and tops coarsely chopped*
> *3 carrots, thinly sliced*
> *¼ teaspoon dried oregano (optional)*
> *¼ cup water*
> *1 pound kielbasa, sliced (see Note)*

1. In a large frying pan, fry bacon until crisp. Drain, reserving 1 tablespoon fat.

2. Add butter to bacon fat in pan; add potatoes, onion, broccoli, carrots, and oregano (if used), and cook, covered, over medium-high heat for 5 minutes, stirring occasionally.

3. Add the water, sliced sausage, and bacon, and cook until vegetables are tender and sausage is heated through (10 minutes).

Note If kielbasa is not available, substitute another smoked sausage.

DARK RYE WITH MELTED CHEESE

> *4 to 8 slices dark rye bread*
> *¼ pound Cheddar, mozzarella, Swiss, jack, or teleme cheese, sliced*

1. Toast bread until firm.

2. Top with cheese and broil until cheese melts. Halve diagonally before serving.

Note Thin slices of tomato or onion make an attractive topping.

SPINACH SALAD WITH LEMON-SOY DRESSING

> *1 bunch spinach, washed and stems removed*
> *6 green onions, sliced (¼ cup)*
> *½ cup sliced radishes*
> *1 cup bean sprouts (optional)*
> *1 can (8 oz) pineapple chunks, drained (reserve 1 tablespoon juice for dressing)*

Lemon-Soy Dressing

> *¼ cup salad oil*
> *2 tablespoons lemon juice*
> *2 tablespoons soy sauce*
> *1 tablespoon pineapple juice
> Half a garlic clove, minced*

1. Chop or tear spinach into bite-sized pieces. Toss with 2 tablespoons of the Lemon-Soy Dressing.

2. Arrange other vegetables and fruit in groups on top of spinach. Serve remaining dressing on side.

Lemon-Soy Dressing Thoroughly combine oil, lemon juice, soy sauce, pineapple juice, and garlic.

QUICK SKILLET SUPPER

Savory Beans and Sausage

Greek Salad

Garlic Bread

*Beverage suggestion:
Beer*

Two types of sausage go into this stovetop entrée. Top individual portions with slices of Garlic Bread, if you wish. An artfully arranged salad of tomatoes, cucumber, and red onion topped with a feta cheese dressing is a light and refreshing counterpoint to the hearty main dish.

COOKING PLAN

1. *Assemble all ingredients and cooking equipment.*

2. *Slice and chop all ingredients for bean dish.*

3. *Sauté sausages.*

4. *Meanwhile, mince and grate ingredients for garlic bread spread and mix together.*

5. *Remove sausages; sauté onion and garlic.*

6. *Add remaining ingredients to bean dish.*

7. *Prepare salad and dressing.*

8. *Preheat broiler.*

9. *Slice bread and spread with seasoned butter. Broil.*

To Serve *Place salad on table; serve bean dish and bread.*

SAVORY BEANS AND SAUSAGE

This is a quick and easy version of the traditional cassoulet, a hearty French country favorite made by simmering dried small white beans and a variety of meats slowly for hours.

> 1 tablespoon butter or salad oil
> 1 pound Polish sausage, sliced
> ½ pound hot Italian sausage, sliced
> 1 cup chopped red or yellow onion
> 1 clove garlic, minced or pressed
> 1 can (54 oz) pork and beans
> ¼ cup white wine
> ¼ teaspoon each *freshly ground black pepper and dried thyme*
> 2 pinches rosemary (crumbled between fingers)
> 1 small bay leaf
> Green onion, diced pimiento, and rosemary sprigs (for garnish; optional)

1. In a large frying pan or heavy saucepan, heat butter; add sausages and sauté until browned. Remove and drain, reserving 1 tablespoon fat.

2. Add onion and garlic to pan and sauté until soft. Add pork and beans, wine, and spices; mix in sausage; and simmer 15 minutes.

3. Garnish if desired.

GREEK SALAD

> 2 fully ripe tomatoes, sliced
> 1 cucumber, thinly sliced
> 1 medium red onion, thinly sliced
> Juice of 1 lemon
> 2 to 3 tablespoons olive oil
> ½ pound feta cheese, crumbled
> Salt and freshly ground black pepper
> Greek olives (for garnish; optional)

1. Top tomatoes with cucumber and onion slices.

2. Mix together lemon juice, olive oil, and cheese; season to taste.

3. Pour dressing over salad; garnish with olives if desired.

GARLIC BREAD

> Half a loaf sweet or sourdough French bread
> ½ cup butter, softened
> 2 or 3 cloves garlic, minced or pressed
> ¼ cup each *minced parsley and freshly grated Parmesan cheese*

1. Preheat broiler.

2. Slice bread to desired thickness.

3. Mix together butter, garlic, parsley, and cheese; spread evenly over slices.

4. Broil slices on cookie sheet until topping is golden and bubbly.

menu

CURRY IN A HURRY

Curried Lamb and Vegetables

Bulgur Wheat

*Endive-and-Mushroom Salad With
Sherried Mustard Dressing*

*Wine suggestion:
Beaujolais*

The ground lamb in this curry cooks faster than the traditional lamb cubes. Serve it with a variety of colorful condiments for diners to add to taste: raisins, shredded coconut, chutney, peanuts or sliced almonds, and yogurt. The bulgur provides a good foil to the spicy curry.

COOKING PLAN

1. *Assemble all ingredients and cooking equipment.*

2. *Sauté bulgur; add liquid and reduce heat.*

3. *Chop and measure ingredients for curried lamb.*

4. *Begin cooking curried lamb.*

5. *Prepare salad and dressing.*

6. *Assemble and chop desired condiments.*

To Serve *Place condiments and salad on table. Top bulgur with curried lamb; garnish.*

CURRIED LAMB AND VEGETABLES

> 1 *tablespoon butter*
> 1 *to 3 teaspoons curry powder*
> 1 *teaspoon grated fresh ginger root or ¼ teaspoon ground ginger*
> 2 *or 3 cloves garlic, minced*
> 1 *medium red onion, chopped*
> 1 *pound ground lamb*
> ½ *pound (20 medium) mushrooms, sliced*
>   *Half a green pepper, seeded and chopped*
> 1 *stalk celery, diced*
> ¼ *cup grated carrot*
>   *Lime wedges (for garnish)*

1. In a large, heavy frying pan over medium-high heat, melt butter. Add curry powder, ginger, garlic, and onion, and sauté 30 seconds.

2. Add lamb and brown lightly. Stir in mushrooms, pepper, and celery. Cook until tender (6 to 8 minutes).

3. Serve on bulgur, topped with grated carrot. Garnish with limes.

BULGUR WHEAT

> 2 *tablespoons vegetable oil*
> 1 *cup bulgur wheat*
> 2 *cups hot water or 1 cup each chicken broth and hot water*
>   *Salt and pepper*

1. In a large frying pan heat oil. Add bulgur and sauté until golden.

2. Add hot liquid. Salt and pepper to taste. Bring to a boil over high heat. Cover; reduce heat. Simmer until liquid is absorbed (about 15 minutes).

ENDIVE-AND-MUSHROOM SALAD WITH SHERRIED MUSTARD DRESSING

> 12 *medium or 8 large mushrooms, washed and stems trimmed*
> 2 *heads endive or 1 head escarole, torn*

Sherried Mustard Dressing

> 2 *green onions, chopped*
> ½ *cup plain yogurt*
> 1½ *teaspoons Dijon mustard*
> 1 *to 2 tablespoons sherry*

1. Arrange mushrooms on endive.

2. Spoon Sherried Mustard Dressing over salad.

Sherried Mustard Dressing Mix onion, yogurt, mustard, and sherry.

menu

MEAT AND POTATOES WITH A DIFFERENCE

Herbed Lamb Patties

Matchstick Potatoes

Carrot Purée

Sliced Beefsteak Tomatoes

Wine suggestion:
Merlot

These tasty broiled patties are made of ground lamb rather than beef; a traditional accompaniment would be mint sauce. The potatoes are matchstick-sized French fries. Serve them with a carrot purée flavored with sherry and spices, and vine-ripened beefsteak tomatoes.

COOKING PLAN

1. *Assemble all ingredients and cooking equipment.*

2. *Chop and measure ingredients for lamb patties. Sauté onion; form patties and set aside.*

3. *Slice potatoes and carrots.*

4. *Steam carrots and heat water for potatoes.*

5. *Slice tomatoes and top with dressing.*

6. *Parboil potatoes; drain.*

7. *Blend carrots and reheat.*

8. *Pan-fry or broil lamb patties.*

9. *Heat oil for potatoes. Just before turning patties, add test potato to oil.*

10. *Turn patties and fry potatoes.*

To Serve *Drain potatoes on paper towels; salt. Serve patties with carrots and potatoes. Place salad on table.*

HERBED LAMB PATTIES

- 1 tablespoon olive oil
- 1 bunch green onions, sliced
- 1½ to 2 pounds ground lamb
- ¼ teaspoon freshly ground black pepper
- ½ teaspoon dried thyme or basil
- 1 tablespoon minced fresh rosemary or 1 teaspoon dried rosemary, crumbled
- 1 tablespoon minced parsley
- 2 teaspoons lemon juice
  Rosemary sprigs (for garnish)

1. In a small frying pan, heat oil. Add green onions. Sauté until limp.

2. In a bowl thoroughly combine sautéed onion with lamb, pepper, herbs, and lemon juice.

3. Form lamb mixture into 4 patties; pan-fry or broil 5 minutes per side, or until done to taste.

4. Garnish with rosemary sprigs.

Nutted Lamb Patties With

Bacon In a small frying pan, partially cook 4 slices bacon; drain and set aside, reserving 1 tablespoon fat in pan. Complete steps 1 and 2, substituting bacon fat for oil and adding ⅓ cup chopped nutmeats to ground lamb with onions and seasonings. Form into 4 patties. Broil first side 5 minutes. Turn patties and broil 3 minutes longer. Top each with a slice of Cheddar cheese and a bacon slice. Broil 2 to 3 minutes longer or until cheese melts and bacon is crisp.

MATCHSTICK POTATOES

3 large potatoes, scrubbed
  and sliced into matchstick-
  sized pieces
Vegetable oil
Salt to taste

1. In a medium saucepan bring to a boil enough water to just cover potatoes; add potatoes and parboil 2 minutes. Drain on paper towels.

2. Pour a ¼-inch layer of oil into a large skillet; heat until oil is hot but not smoking. (A piece of potato should rise immediately to the surface and bob about.) Add potatoes and fry until golden (4 to 5 minutes).

3. Drain on paper towels. Sprinkle with salt.

CARROT PURÉE

2 tablespoons butter
1 pound carrots, peeled and
  sliced thinly (3 cups)
2 tablespoons water
1 cup whipping cream
1 to 2 tablespoons dry sherry
¼ teaspoon each nutmeg
  and cinnamon

1. In a large skillet melt butter. Add carrots and the water and steam, covered, until soft (5 to 8 minutes).

2. In blender or food processor container, combine carrots with whipping cream, sherry, nutmeg, and cinnamon; blend until smooth. Reheat.

SLICED BEEFSTEAK TOMATOES

3 large beefsteak tomatoes
⅓ cup olive oil
¼ cup lemon juice
1 tablespoon each minced
  fresh or ½ teaspoon dried
  basil and rosemary

1. Slice tomatoes.

2. Whisk together olive oil, lemon juice, and herbs and pour over tomatoes. Let stand at room temperature until serving.

---

menu

SPRING LAMB CELEBRATION

Loin Lamb Chops With Juniper Sauce

Couscous With Mushrooms

Brussels Sprouts

Wine suggestion:
Côtes-du-Rhône or
Cabernet Sauvignon

Celebrate the first daffodils of spring with broiled loin lamb chops topped with the unusual flavor of Juniper Sauce. If the weather is warm enough, grill the chops rather than broiling them. Couscous tossed with green onions, pine nuts, and mushrooms adds a festive touch.

COOKING PLAN

1. Assemble all ingredients and cooking equipment.

2. Preheat broiler.

3. Wash and score sprouts; heat water. Mince garlic, crush berries, and measure other ingredients for chops and sauce.

4. Slice onions and mushrooms for couscous. Chop onion for sprouts.

5. Add sprouts to boiling water.

6. Season chops and broil. Prepare sauce.

7. Turn chops, adding drippings to sauce.

8. Heat broth for couscous and prepare dish.

9. Drain sprouts; sauté onion and return sprouts to pan.

To Serve *Drizzle chops with a little sauce; offer remainder separately. Fluff couscous and serve sprouts.*

LOIN LAMB CHOPS WITH JUNIPER SAUCE

Thinner chops, such as round-bone or shoulder, can also be prepared in this way—simply reduce the broiling time to 4 or 5 minutes per side. Juniper berries are an intriguing alternative to the classic mint sauce.

4 loin lamb chops (¾ to
  1 in. thick)
2 cloves garlic, pressed
1 tablespoon juniper berries,
  crushed
  Salt and freshly ground
  pepper

Juniper Sauce

½ cup beef broth
⅔ cup dry red wine
1 clove garlic, minced
1 tablespoon juniper berries,
  crushed
1 tablespoon red currant jelly
  Drippings from lamb chops
1 tablespoon cornstarch
2 tablespoons water
  Salt and freshly ground
  pepper to taste

1. Rub chops with a paste of the garlic, juniper berries, and salt and pepper to taste.

2. Line broiler with foil to collect drippings, which should be added to sauce. Broil chops 4 inches from heat source until done to taste (6 to 8 minutes per side for slightly pink, juicy meat).

3. While chops cook, prepare Juniper Sauce.

4. Spoon a little sauce over each chop; serve remainder separately.

Juniper Sauce In a small saucepan over medium-high heat, bring broth, wine, garlic, and berries to a boil. Reduce heat and simmer 6 minutes. Stir in red currant jelly and drippings from chops. In a small bowl blend cornstarch with the water; stir into sauce. Bring sauce to a boil, and season to taste with salt and pepper.

COUSCOUS WITH MUSHROOMS

> 3 cups chicken broth
> 2 cups quick-cooking couscous
> 3 green onions, thinly sliced
> 3 to 4 tablespoons toasted pine nuts or sliced almonds
> ½ cup thinly sliced fresh mushrooms
> Minced parsley (for garnish)

1. In a large saucepan bring broth to a boil; add couscous, onions, nuts, and mushrooms; stir.

2. Immediately remove from heat, cover, and let stand until liquid is absorbed (5 minutes).

3. Serve garnished with parsley.

BRUSSELS SPROUTS

> 1 pound Brussels sprouts
> 2 tablespoons butter
> ¼ cup finely chopped red or yellow onion
> Salt and freshly ground pepper

1. In a large saucepan bring to a boil enough water to just cover sprouts.

2. Trim stem ends of sprouts and cut an X in stem of each to speed cooking.

3. Add sprouts to boiling water, reduce heat, and simmer, uncovered, until tender (10 to 15 minutes). Drain and set aside.

4. In the same saucepan melt butter. Add onion and cook until soft (5 minutes), covering pan to speed cooking.

5. Add sprouts, toss to coat with butter, reheat, and season to taste.

DINNER PROVENCE STYLE

Lamb Chops Provençale

Creamed Chard

Glazed Parsnips

Wine suggestion:
Beaujolais

The sauce for the broiled lamb chops features tomatoes and garlic, traditional ingredients in the cuisine of Provence, France. Creamed Chard, sauced with cream cheese, and parsnips in a buttery brown-sugar glaze feature vegetables that are both delicious and low in cost.

COOKING PLAN

1. *Assemble all ingredients and cooking equipment.*

2. *Chop ingredients for sauce. Wash and chop chard. Clean parsnips.*

3. *Preheat broiler, and heat water for parsnips.*

4. *Sauté vegetables for sauce. Add remaining ingredients and simmer.*

5. *Warm holding dish for chard in 200° F oven.*

6. *Cook parsnips. Place chops in broiler.*

7. *Check chops and turn when ready.*

8. *Cook chard.*

9. *Drain parsnips and glaze. Put chard in warmed dish and make sauce. Season chard.*

To Serve *Spoon sauce over chops. Serve vegetables.*

LAMB CHOPS PROVENÇALE

This French country sauce is also excellent with pork or chicken, or as a topping for pasta or omelets. If you have a few extra minutes, double the recipe and freeze half for future use.

> 4 loin, round-bone, or shoulder lamb chops, trimmed

Sauce Provençale

> 1 tablespoon olive oil
> 1 medium onion, finely chopped
> 2 cloves garlic, minced or pressed
> 1 can (16 oz) whole tomatoes, drained
> 1 green pepper, seeded and sliced
> ½ cup dry red wine

1. Broil chops 4 inches from heat source 4 to 8 minutes per side, depending on thickness.

2. Top with Sauce Provençale.

Sauce Provençale In a large frying pan heat oil. Add onion and garlic and sauté briefly. Crush tomatoes and add to pan; sauté briefly. Add green pepper and wine and simmer 15 minutes. Serve over broiled chops.

CREAMED CHARD

> 2 tablespoons butter
> 2 bunches chard (leaves only), washed and chopped
> 2 tablespoons water
> 1 package (3 oz) cream cheese, at room temperature
> ⅛ teaspoon nutmeg
> Salt and freshly ground pepper to taste

1. In a large skillet over medium-high heat, melt butter. Add chard, the water, and cream cheese, broken into chunks.

2. Cover and cook until chard is tender (about 4 minutes).

3. Add nutmeg and salt and pepper to taste; mix well.

GLAZED PARSNIPS

> 1½ pounds (8 to 10 medium) parsnips, trimmed and peeled
> 2 tablespoons each butter and brandy
> 1 tablespoon brown sugar or honey

1. In a large skillet in boiling water to cover, cook parsnips just until tender (10 to 15 minutes). Drain.

2. Add butter, brandy, and brown sugar to skillet. Sauté parsnips over medium-high heat, shaking skillet occasionally until glazed on all sides.

menu

PASTA SUPPER

Casserole of Noodles Italian Style

Fruited Romaine Salad

Wine suggestion:
Bardolino or Gamay

This creamy noodle casserole contains onion, mushrooms, herbs, and Parmesan cheese. Toss sliced kiwi fruit and oranges with crisp leaves of romaine for the salad, served with cruets of oil and vinegar for guests to add to taste. A loaf of crusty Italian bread, warmed in a 350° F oven for 10 minutes, makes a delightful accompaniment.

COOKING PLAN

1. *Assemble all ingredients and cooking equipment.*

2. *Heat water for pasta.*

3. *Preheat oven to 375° F.*

4. *Chop parsley, onions, and mushrooms and grate cheese for casserole. Combine with other ingredients.*

5. *As soon as water boils, add pasta.*

6. *Drain pasta and assemble casserole. Place in oven.*

7. *Make salad and mince parsley for casserole garnish.*

To Serve *Garnish casserole. Place salad, cruets, and casserole on table.*

CASSEROLE OF NOODLES ITALIAN STYLE

You can add almost anything to this basic pasta casserole: heated diced leftover beef or chicken, baby shrimp, half-strips of crisp bacon, or cooked vegetables such as broccoli, peas, or carrots.

4 quarts water
2 teaspoons salt
1 pound medium noodles
3 eggs, well beaten
¼ cup whipping cream
5 tablespoons minced parsley
¼ cup minced onion
1 cup freshly grated Parmesan cheese
½ pound (20 medium) mushrooms, sliced
1 tablespoon fines herbes
Salt and pepper to taste

1. Preheat oven to 375° F.

2. In a large pot bring the water and the 2 teaspoons salt to a boil. Add noodles and cook until they are al dente (about 5 to 7 minutes); drain.

3. Meanwhile, combine eggs, whipping cream, ¼ cup of the parsley, onion, cheese, mushrooms, herbs, and seasonings.

4. Place noodles in a greased casserole dish; pour sauce over noodles and stir to mix.

5. Bake 20 minutes; garnish with reserved 1 tablespoon parsley.

FRUITED ROMAINE SALAD

1 head romaine
2 large carrots
2 oranges
2 or 3 kiwi fruit
Cruets of oil and vinegar

1. Wash and chop or tear romaine in bite-sized pieces.

2. Scrub carrots and slice into long, thin strips using a vegetable peeler.

3. Peel and slice oranges and kiwi fruit.

4. Arrange carrot strips and fruits on lettuce. Serve with oil and vinegar.

VEGETARIAN FAVORITE

Eggplant Parmigiana

Vermicelli

Baked Mushrooms

Wine suggestion:
Trebbiano
or Valpolicella

Eggplant Parmigiana, a meatless entrée, is both delicious and economical. The mushrooms are baked in foil, then served topped with sour cream for a mouth-watering side dish.

COOKING PLAN

1. Assemble all ingredients and cooking equipment.

2. Preheat oven to 450°F. Heat water in steamer.

3. Chop vegetables for sauce and sauté.

4. Prepare mushrooms; place in oven.

5. Slice eggplant and place in steamer.

6. Add remaining ingredients to sauce. Heat water for vermicelli.

7. Blot eggplant; coat and sauté.

8. Slice cheese; assemble eggplant dish.

9. Add vermicelli to boiling water.

To Serve *Drain vermicelli and top with eggplant and sauce. Garnish mushrooms with sour cream.*

EGGPLANT PARMIGIANA

This hearty dish is a vegetarian classic. The sauce goes well with many pasta, egg, and meat dishes.

> 1 large eggplant, unpeeled
> ½ cup flour
> 1 egg, beaten with ¼ cup milk
> ½ cup dry bread crumbs, wheat germ, or cracker meal
> ½ cup olive oil
> ½ pound mozzarella or Swiss cheese, sliced
> Freshly grated Parmesan cheese (optional)

Parmigiana Sauce

> 1 tablespoon olive oil
> 1 small red onion, chopped
> 1 large clove garlic, minced
> ¼ cup diced green pepper (optional)
> 1 can (28 oz) Italian plum tomatoes
> 1 tablespoon minced parsley (optional)
> ½ teaspoon each *dried basil, thyme, and oregano*

1. Wash eggplant and cut into ½-inch-thick slices. Steam over boiling water for 5 minutes. Press each slice firmly between paper towels to remove moisture.

2. Coat each slice well, first with flour, then with egg-milk mixture, and finally with bread crumbs.

3. Divide oil between 2 large frying pans; Add eggplant and sauté over medium-high heat until golden brown on both sides.

4. Top each eggplant slice with a cheese slice. Cover pans and cook over low heat until cheese melts (5 minutes). Serve on vermicelli, topped with Parmigiana Sauce.

Parmigiana Sauce In a large frying pan, heat oil. Add onion, garlic, and green pepper and sauté until softened. Add tomatoes (breaking up with a fork) and their liquid and the herbs to pan. Simmer, uncovered, until liquid is reduced (10 to 15 minutes). Serve sauce over the eggplant and vermicelli.

VERMICELLI

2 quarts water
1 teaspoon salt
8 ounces Italian vermicelli
1 tablespoon oil

1. In a large pot bring the water and salt to a boil.

2. Add vermicelli and oil and cook, uncovered, until pasta is al dente (3 to 5 minutes). Drain.

BAKED MUSHROOMS

¾ pound (30 medium) mushrooms
5 tablespoons minced parsley
2 to 3 tablespoons dry sherry
Salt and freshly ground pepper
Sour cream

1. Preheat oven to 450° F.

2. Rinse mushrooms, trim stem ends, and halve. Place on piece of foil large enough to enclose them completely.

3. Top with ¼ cup of the parsley, the sherry, and salt and pepper to taste. Seal package tightly so that juices won't leak.

4. Bake until tender (20 minutes).

5. Top each serving with a dollop of sour cream, or place mushrooms in serving dish and fold in enough sour cream to coat them. Garnish with remaining 1 tablespoon parsley.

Menu

A PASTA POTPOURRI

Pasta With Sauce
Garden Patch Green Salad
Rosemary Loaf
Wine suggestion:
Gamay Beaujolais or Verdicchio

The wide range of pasta shapes and the almost unlimited number of sauces make pasta one of the most versatile foods around. Here are six sauces you're sure to like. Pictured here is spinach fettucine with Dr. Jack's Curried Cream Sauce, a smooth blend of cream, curry, cheese, and tiny shrimp. Garden Patch Green Salad goes well with any pasta dish.

COOKING PLAN

1. *Assemble all ingredients and cooking equipment.*

2. *Chop, mince, or grate ingredients for sauce of your choice. If sauce must simmer, prepare now.*

3. *Wash and slice salad ingredients and assemble salad.*

4. *Heat water for pasta. Preheat broiler.*

5. *Prepare rosemary loaf but do not broil.*

6. *Cook pasta. If sauce does not require simmering, prepare now.*

7. *Place bread in broiler.*

8. *Drain pasta, and toss or top with sauce.*

To Serve *Dress salad, remove bread from broiler, and garnish pasta.*

PASTA WITH SAUCE

4 quarts water
2 teaspoons salt
2 tablespoons olive oil
1 pound spaghetti, noodles, or macaroni
Pasta sauce (recipes follow)

1. In a large pot, bring the water and salt to a rapid boil. Add oil and then pasta. Return to a boil.

2. Cook pasta, uncovered, until it is al dente (7 to 10 minutes, depending on size and shape). Stir occasionally with a long-handled fork to prevent sticking. Cook fresh pasta according to instructions at point of purchase or according to the pasta recipe.

3. Drain in colander. Do not rinse.

4. Top with your choice of sauce.

Parmesan Sauce In a medium saucepan melt ¼ cup butter. Add 1 cup freshly grated Parmesan cheese, ½ cup half-and-half or evaporated skim milk, and salt and pepper to taste. Pour over cooked pasta. Garnish with minced parsley.

Mushroom Sauce In a large frying pan, heat 2 tablespoons butter or olive oil. Add 1 pound mushrooms, coarsely chopped; ⅓ cup chopped green onion; and 1 or 2 cloves garlic, minced; sauté briefly. Stir in ½ cup white wine or chicken broth, 1 bay leaf, and ½ teaspoon *each* Worcestershire sauce, dried basil, dried oregano, and salt. Simmer 10 to 15 minutes. Pour over cooked pasta. Top with freshly grated Parmesan cheese.

Dr. Jack's Curried Cream Sauce In a medium saucepan melt 2 tablespoons butter. Add 2 tablespoons flour and cook, stirring, until bubbly. Blend in 2 cups half-and-half or evaporated skim milk and ½ to 1 teaspoon curry powder. Bring to a boil and cook until slightly thickened. Fold in ½ to 1 pound tiny shrimp, thawed, and ½ to ¾ cup freshly grated Romano or Parmesan cheese. Pour over cooked pasta.

Joe Cillo's Four-Cheese Favorite Toss ¼ pound *each* Gruyère and Fontina cheese, finely cubed, and 1 cup *each* freshly grated Parmesan and Romano cheese with 2 tablespoons flour. In a heavy-bottomed saucepan, heat ¼ cup butter and 1 cup half-and-half or evaporated skim milk until butter melts. Gradually stir in cheeses and cook over medium heat until sauce is smooth. Add 1 tablespoon chopped fresh basil, rosemary, or thyme *or* 1 teaspoon any dried herb. Pour sauce over cooked pasta and toss quickly with two spoons. Just before serving, toss with an additional ½ to ¾ cup coarsely grated Parmesan cheese.

Sauce Amandine Mix together ⅔ cup coarsely ground dry-roasted almonds, 6 to 8 ounces prosciutto, diced (optional); ¼ cup *each* shredded provolone and Monterey jack cheese; 2 to 3 tablespoons half-and-half or evaporated skim milk beaten with 1 egg; 1 clove garlic, minced; and ½ teaspoon Italian herb seasoning. Return drained pasta to pot, add sauce ingredients, and toss lightly over medium heat until cheese melts. Garnish with black pepper, minced parsley, and chopped almonds.

Italian-Sausage-and-Pepper Sauce In a large frying pan, sauté until browned ½ pound *each* hot and sweet Italian pork sausages (casings removed) *or* 1 pound bulk sausage. Drain all but 1 tablespoon fat. Add 1 green pepper, seeded and cut in strips; ¼ cup sliced red onion; 1 clove garlic, minced; 1 teaspoon dried oregano; ½ teaspoon *each* dried basil and thyme; ½ teaspoon salt; and ¼ teaspoon freshly ground pepper. Sauté until pepper and onion are tender (10 minutes), stirring frequently. Stir in 1 can (28 oz) plum tomatoes (and liquid), breaking up with a fork. Simmer to reduce liquid and heat ingredients through (about 5 minutes). Pour over drained pasta. Top with grated Parmesan cheese.

GARDEN PATCH GREEN SALAD

  2 heads butter or red leaf lettuce, escarole, or spinach, or *a combination, torn or chopped in bite-sized pieces*
  3 ripe tomatoes, sliced
  1 cucumber, sliced
  1 zucchini, thinly sliced
  2 carrots, grated or cut in sticks
  1½ cups sliced fresh mushrooms
  ½ cup seedless grapes, or
  1 or 2 kiwi fruit, peeled and sliced, or
  1 red or yellow apple, cored, thinly sliced, and tossed with a little lemon juice
     Salad dressing of choice

Gently toss ingredients in a bowl. Dress immediately before serving.

ROSEMARY LOAF

  1 round (1 lb) French or Italian loaf
  ½ cup butter, softened
  1 tablespoon chopped fresh or 1 teaspoon dried rosemary, crumbled
  2 to 3 tablespoons minced parsley
  ¼ cup grated Romano or Parmesan cheese

1. Preheat broiler.

2. Slice bread.

3. Thoroughly combine butter, rosemary, parsley, and cheese. Spread evenly over slices.

4. Broil until topping is bubbly and golden brown.

ONE-POT CAJUN DINNER

Jambalaya One-Pot Meal
Citrus Salad With Yogurt Dressing

Wine suggestion:
Rioja Riserva or
Pinot Noir Blanc

Although there are a number of ingredients to prepare, this New Orleans–style dish needs no attention while it cooks, leaving you free to prepare the salad. Rice is a versatile basis for a one-pot meal. Try one of the variations, or invent a recipe of your own.

COOKING PLAN

1. *Assemble all ingredients and cooking equipment.*

2. *Chop vegetables for jambalaya and sauté, adding to pan as they are chopped.*

3. *Slice meats and clean shrimp.*

4. *Add remaining ingredients to jambalaya and cover.*

5. *Prepare salad and dressing.*

6. *Add shrimp to jambalaya.*

To Serve *Dress salad. Gently toss jambalaya and garnish it.*

JAMBALAYA ONE-POT MEAL

  2 *tablespoons olive oil*
  2 *cloves garlic, minced or pressed*
  ½ *cup chopped onion*
  1 *stalk celery, sliced*
  1 *medium green pepper, seeded and cut in strips*
  1 *cup long-grain white rice*
  1 *can (16 oz) stewed tomatoes*
  1 *cup water*
  ⅛ *teaspoon hot-pepper sauce (optional)*
  ½ *cup chopped cooked ham (optional)*
  8 *thin slices chorizo or other spicy hard sausage*
  1 *teaspoon dried thyme or oregano*
  1 *teaspoon salt*
    Freshly ground pepper
  1 *pound medium-sized raw (deveined) or frozen shrimp*
    Lemon slices and minced parsley (for garnish)

1. In a large frying or paella pan, heat oil. Add garlic, onion, celery, and green pepper and sauté just until softened (about 3 minutes).

2. Add rice, tomatoes and their juice, the water, hot-pepper sauce and ham (if used), chorizo, and seasonings. Bring to a boil, cover, reduce heat, and simmer 15 minutes.

3. Quickly add shrimp, cover, and cook 5 minutes longer, or until rice is tender and shrimp have turned pink.

4. Toss with a fork. Garnish with lemons and parsley.

Paella One-Pot Meal In a large frying or paella pan, heat 2 tablespoons olive oil. Add 2 cloves garlic, minced; ½ cup chopped onion; and 2 hot or mild chorizos, casings removed and broken into pieces; sauté 3 to 5 minutes. Add 1 cup long-grain white rice; 2 cups chicken broth; 1 whole boned chicken breast, cut in strips or bite-sized pieces; ⅛ teaspoon saffron *or* ¼ teaspoon turmeric; 1 teaspoon salt. Pepper to taste. Bring to a boil, cover, reduce heat, and simmer 15 minutes. Then add 10

ounces frozen petite peas *or* 1 can (16 oz) artichoke hearts, drained, and 1 pound medium-sized raw (deveined) or frozen shrimp. Cover and cook 5 minutes longer. You can also add 8 fresh clams or mussels with the shrimp (reduce shrimp to ½ pound). Cook shellfish until shells open.

Gingered Chicken One-Pot Meal

In a large frying or paella pan, heat 2 tablespoons oil. Add 1 clove garlic, minced; ½ cup chopped onion; 1 cup sliced fresh mushrooms; and 1 tablespoon grated fresh ginger root; sauté just until softened (3 minutes). Add 1 cup long-grain white rice; 2 cups chicken broth (or 1¾ cups broth and ¼ cup mandarin juice); 2 whole boned chicken breasts, cut in strips or bite-sized pieces; ½ cup toasted slivered almonds or chopped walnuts; ½ cup raisins; 1 teaspoon salt. Pepper to taste. Bring to a boil, cover, reduce heat, and simmer 20 minutes. Add 1 can (11½ oz) mandarin orange segments, drained, after 15 minutes.

CITRUS SALAD WITH YOGURT DRESSING

  2 *small heads butter or Bibb lettuce*
  1 *avocado, peeled, seeded, and sliced*
  1 *orange, peeled, seeded, and sliced, or 1 can (11½ oz) mandarin orange segments, drained*

Yogurt Dressing

  1 *cup plain yogurt*
  ¼ *cup orange juice*
  2 *teaspoons grated orange rind*
    Dash ground cloves
    Confectioners' sugar to taste

Wash and dry lettuce leaves. Arrange on individual plates. Top with avocado, orange slices, and dressing.

Yogurt Dressing Mix ingredients. Let stand for flavors to blend.

VEGETARIAN STIR-FRY

Stir-Fried Vegetable Delight

Herbed Brown Rice

Wine suggestion:
Chenin Blanc or Gewürztraminer

Stir-frying is a natural for the 30-minute cook. This colorful meatless dish features a mixture of vegetables, including peppers, green beans, mushrooms, and bok choy, with tofu providing the protein. Be sure to have all of the vegetables prepared before you begin cooking—it goes together quickly! Prepare a mixture of cheese, whole grain crackers, and sliced fruit on a cutting board as a light dessert.

COOKING PLAN

1. *Assemble all ingredients and cooking equipment.*

2. *Start rice.*

3. *Slice, chop, and mince all vegetables.*

4. *Stir-fry vegetables.*

To Serve *Spoon vegetables over rice. Arrange side dishes and pour the wine.*

STIR-FRIED VEGETABLE DELIGHT

- 3 tablespoons peanut oil
- 1 to 3 cloves garlic, minced or pressed
- 2 teaspoons grated fresh ginger root
- 1 small red onion, sliced
- 2 green or red peppers, or 1 of each, seeded and diced
- ¼ pound green beans, sliced diagonally in 1-inch lengths
- 1 carrot, coarsely grated
- ¾ pound (30 medium) mushrooms, sliced
- 1 small bunch bok choy or chard
- 1 zucchini, sliced
- ¼ pound tofu, cubed
- 1½ teaspoons dried basil
- ½ teaspoon dried thyme
- 2 tablespoons minced parsley
- 1 teaspoon lemon juice
- 2 to 3 tablespoons soy sauce, or to taste

1. In a large wok or frying pan, heat oil, garlic, and ginger.

2. Add onion, peppers, beans, and carrot. Stir-fry over high heat 4 minutes.

3. Add mushrooms, bok choy, zucchini, tofu, and herbs. Pour lemon juice and soy sauce over vegetables and stir-fry until tender-crisp (4 to 5 minutes). Serve over rice.

HERBED BROWN RICE

- 2 cups water
- 1 tablespoon butter
- 1 cup short-grain brown rice
- 1½ teaspoons dried basil
- ¼ teaspoon dried thyme
- 1 teaspoon minced parsley

1. In a medium saucepan bring water, butter, and rice to a boil. Add basil, thyme, and parsley; stir once.

2. Cover, reduce heat. Simmer until water is absorbed (25 to 30 minutes).

SUPER TACO SALAD

Taco Salad

Chili Bread

Beverage suggestion:
Mexican beer

Main-dish Taco Salad makes a great light meal with a Mexican flair. Try topping it with red onions, sour cream or plain yogurt, ripe olives, and salsa for added flavor. The Chili Bread is a new twist on that old favorite, garlic bread.

COOKING PLAN

1. *Assemble all ingredients and cooking equipment.*

2. *Clean and cut all vegetables for salad; shred cheese. Chop cilantro.*

3. *Brown ground beef.*

4. *Prepare toppings for salads.*

5. *Prepare chili bread. Preheat broiler.*

6. *Assemble salads.*

7. *Place bread in broiler.*

To Serve *Add toppings of your choice to salads. Remove bread from broiler and serve.*

TACO SALAD

½ to ¾ pound ground beef

½ to 1 teaspoon chili powder

⅛ teaspoon garlic powder

½ to 1 teaspoon dried red chile flakes (optional)

1 head curly green leaf or butter lettuce, separated into leaves

1 head iceberg lettuce, shredded (8 cups)

3 tomatoes, cut in wedges

1 or 2 avocados, peeled, seeded, and sliced (12 slices each)

1 can (16 oz) kidney beans, drained

1 cup shredded Monterey jack or Cheddar cheese

1 cup tortilla chips
   Optional toppings: red onion rings, ripe olives, sour cream or plain yogurt, salsa

1. In a medium frying pan, brown meat with seasonings. Keep warm or allow to cool to room temperature.

2. To build individual salads: Place 4 lettuce leaves in each bowl. Mound one fourth of the shredded lettuce in center of leaves. Alternate tomato wedges and avocado slices around base of mound. Top each with one fourth of the beans, beef, and cheese. Surround with one fourth of the chips. Add your choice of toppings if desired.

CHILI BREAD

½ cup butter, softened

½ teaspoon chili powder

1 loaf French bread, sliced

¼ cup chopped cilantro (optional)

1. Preheat broiler.

2. Combine butter and chili powder and spread on bread slices. Sprinkle with cilantro if desired.

3. Broil until golden (2 to 3 minutes).

SOUP AND A SANDWICH

Italian Knife-and-Fork Soup

Antipasto Pita Sandwiches

Wine suggestion:
Barbaresco

This simple but hearty supper features a soup so full of good ingredients that it's practically a stew. Sweet and hot sausages, potatoes, peppers, and onion cook in a rich tomato-and-herb-flavored broth. To go with it, a choice of tasty fillings to serve in warm pita breads.

COOKING PLAN

1. *Assemble all ingredients and cooking equipment.*

2. *Preheat oven to 350° F.*

3. *Quarter sausages and cook. Meanwhile, slice or mince vegetables for soup.*

4. *Brown sausages.*

5. *Remove sausages and sauté vegetables for soup.*

6. *Place pita bread in oven.*

7. *Add liquids and sausages and let soup simmer.*

8. *Prepare filling for sandwiches.*

9. *Shred or slice vegetables and cheese for sandwiches. Place toppings for soup in bowls.*

10. *Remove pitas from oven and assemble sandwiches.*

To Serve *Place sandwiches and toppings for soup on table. Ladle soup into bowls.*

ITALIAN KNIFE-AND-FORK SOUP

> ½ pound each *sweet and hot Italian pork sausages, quartered*
> ½ cup water
> 2 tablespoons olive oil
> 4 potatoes, thinly sliced
> 1 each *large red and green pepper, seeded and cut into strips*
> 1 small red or yellow onion, sliced
> 3 or 4 cloves garlic, minced or pressed
> 1 teaspoon dried oregano
> ½ teaspoon dried rosemary, crumbled
> ¾ cup tomato paste
> 4 cups beef or chicken broth
> Salt and freshly ground pepper
> Toppings: freshly grated Parmesan cheese, minced green onions, croutons (optional)

1. In a large covered pot over medium-high heat, simmer sausages in ¼ cup of the water 4 minutes.

2. Uncover pot, discard water, increase heat, and brown sausages on all sides (about 5 minutes). Remove sausages with slotted spoon and set aside. Discard fat and wipe out pot.

3. Heat olive oil in pot. Add potatoes, peppers, onion, garlic, oregano, and rosemary and sauté 5 minutes.

4. Stir in tomato paste, remaining ¼ cup water, broth, and reserved sausages. Cover and cook 10 minutes. Season to taste and serve with choice of toppings.

ANTIPASTO PITA SANDWICHES

For a quick dinner, pita (or pocket) bread holds both a salad and the sandwich filling of your choice.

> 4 pitas
> 1 clove garlic, minced (optional)
> ¼ cup mayonnaise
> 8 lettuce leaves
> 1 cup shredded lettuce
> 8 slices provolone or mozzarella cheese
> 8 slices each *tomato and cucumber*
> Choice of fillings:
> Tiny cooked shrimp mixed with a little olive oil and lemon juice
> Marinated artichoke hearts or mushrooms
> Mixed pickled vegetables
> Olives
> Thinly sliced prosciutto

1. Wrap pitas in a dampened towel and warm in 350° F oven for 10 minutes.

2. Mix garlic (if used) with mayonnaise. Halve pitas and spread insides with mayonnaise.

3. Place 1 lettuce leaf and 2 tablespoons shredded lettuce in each half; top with 1 slice each cheese, tomato, and cucumber, and add filling of your choice.

SUPPER ALFRESCO

*Shrimp Salad Sandwich
With Fresh Fruit*

Cream of Watercress Soup

*Wine suggestion:
Chenin Blanc*

This summer menu practically begs to be served outdoors. An open-face Shrimp Salad Sandwich served surrounded with fresh fruit is a refreshing treat after a long, hot day. You will probably want to make Cream of Watercress Soup ahead and chill it, but it can also be served hot.

COOKING PLAN

1. Assemble all ingredients and cooking equipment.

2. Chop onion and watercress for soup, reserving sprigs for garnish. Chop onion for sandwich filling and cut up vegetables and fruits. If you are using fresh juice, squeeze lemon. Slice lemons for garnish.

3. Prepare filling for sandwiches.

4. Prepare soup and let simmer.

5. Assemble sandwiches.

6. Blend soup; reheat if necessary.

To Serve *Arrange fruit on plates with sandwiches. Garnish soup and sandwiches.*

SHRIMP SALAD SANDWICH WITH FRESH FRUIT

- 3 tablespoons each *softened cream cheese and mayonnaise*
- 1 teaspoon *lemon juice*
- ⅛ to ¼ teaspoon *dried dillweed*
- 2 tablespoons *chopped green onion*
- 1 pound *small cooked, peeled shrimp*
- 8 slices *sourdough French bread Mayonnaise*
- 8 leaves *curly green leaf lettuce*
- 8 slices *tomato*
- 8 slices *avocado*
- 8 slices *cantaloupe Half a basket fresh strawberries, raspberries, or blackberries Lemon wheels and dill sprigs (for garnish)*

1. Mix cream cheese, 3 tablespoons mayonnaise, lemon juice, and dillweed. Fold in onion and shrimp.

2. Spread mayonnaise on bread slices; top with a lettuce leaf.

3. Divide the shrimp salad evenly among 4 slices. Top each of the remaining slices with 2 tomato slices, and then with 2 avocado slices.

4. Arrange 2 cantaloupe slices, berries, and lemon wheels on plate. Garnish shrimp salad with dill sprigs.

CREAM OF WATERCRESS SOUP

- ¼ cup *butter*
- 1 bunch *green onions, chopped*
- 2 tablespoons each *flour and nonfat dry milk*
- 1 quart *whole milk, at room temperature*
- 2 bunches *watercress, coarsely chopped (reserve 4 sprigs for garnish)*
- ⅛ teaspoon *nutmeg*
- 1 teaspoon *lemon juice Salt and freshly ground pepper Yogurt (optional) and lemon wheels (for garnish)*

1. In a medium saucepan, heat butter. Add onions and sauté briefly.

2. Tilt pan, stir in flour and dry milk, blend, and cook until bubbly.

3. Gradually add whole milk. Cook, stirring continuously, until soup comes to a boil and thickens. Reduce heat to simmer.

4. Add chopped watercress, nutmeg, and lemon juice. Cover and simmer 3 minutes.

5. Remove soup from heat. Whirl in blender, until smooth. Season to taste. Reheat or serve soup chilled.

6. Garnish with a dollop of yogurt, lemon wheel, and a watercress sprig.

CURRIED CHICKEN SALAD

Cashew Chicken Salad in
Fluted Cantaloupe Halves

Wine suggestion:
Chardonnay

Raisins, cashews, chutney, and curry powder turn chicken salad into a gourmet treat. Serve the salad in edible bowls made of fluted cantaloupe halves for a light and refreshing meal. To accompany it, warm half a dozen croissants or a small loaf of nut bread in a 350° F oven for 10 minutes.

COOKING PLAN

1. *Assemble all ingredients and cooking equipment.*

2. *Wash and chop vegetables and fruit for salad. Wash grapes.*

3. *Combine salad ingredients and chill.*

4. *Flute and seed cantaloupes; refrigerate.*

To Serve *Fill cantaloupe halves with salad; garnish.*

CASHEW CHICKEN SALAD IN FLUTED CANTALOUPE HALVES

This fruited salad, which uses cooked chicken, is ideal for a hot summer evening.

 3 *cups cold cooked, shredded chicken (ideally, 3 whole breasts, skinned and boned)*
 ½ *cup cashews, coarsely chopped*
 ¼ *cup each sliced celery and green onion*
 1 *small tart green apple, cored and diced*
 2 *tablespoons raisins*
 2 *to 3 tablespoons chutney*
 ¾ *to 1 cup mayonnaise*
 2 *teaspoons curry powder*
 2 *teaspoons lemon juice*
  Cayenne and garlic salt
 2 *small cantaloupes*
  Paprika and 4 small bunches red or green grapes (for garnish)

1. In a large bowl combine chicken, cashews, celery, green onion, apple, and raisins.

2. Blend chutney, mayonnaise, curry powder, and lemon juice; mix with chicken and season to taste with cayenne and garlic salt. Chill.

3. Flute and seed cantaloupes. Refrigerate until ready to fill.

4. Fill hollows with salad, sprinkle with paprika, and garnish with grapes.

SPANISH-STYLE SUPPER

Gazpacho

Fresh Vegetable Salad With Yogurt-Dill Dressing

Garlic Bread (see page 74)

Beverage suggestion: Mexican beer

Gazpacho, a chilled Spanish soup of chopped vegetables in a spicy tomato juice broth, is low in both cost and calories. Double the recipe so you will have some on hand for lunches or snacks. Served in a mug alongside Garlic Bread and a summery vegetable salad topped with Yogurt-Dill Dressing, it makes a delicious light meal.

COOKING PLAN

1. *Assemble all ingredients and cooking equipment.*

2. *Chop vegetables for soup. Add liquids and chill. Chill bowls for soup.*

3. *Assemble salad. Make dressing and chill.*

4. *Chop toppings for soup and place in small bowls.*

5. *Preheat broiler and prepare garlic bread.*

6. *Put bread in broiler.*

To Serve *Place toppings for soup on table. Dress salad. Remove bread from broiler and ladle soup into bowls.*

GAZPACHO

- 1 large cucumber, peeled and chopped
- 1 red onion, peeled and diced
- 4 large ripe tomatoes, chopped
- 2 or 3 cloves garlic, minced or pressed
- 1 cup chilled chicken broth
- 2 cups chilled vegetable juice cocktail or tomato juice
- 2 tablespons white wine vinegar
- 1 tablespoon olive oil
- 1 teaspoon lemon juice
- ½ teaspoon Worcestershire sauce
- 1 teaspoon each *chili powder and salt*

   Choice of toppings: chopped green onion, chopped green pepper, minced cilantro, sour cream, croutons

1. Combine all ingredients (except toppings). Cover and place in freezer to chill.

2. Serve in chilled bowls with choice of toppings.

FRESH VEGETABLE SALAD WITH YOGURT-DILL DRESSING

- 1 bunch watercress
- 1 cucumber, thinly sliced
- 1 each *carrot and yellow crookneck squash, cut in long, thin strips with a vegetable peeler*
- ¼ cup sliced ripe olives
   Dill sprigs (for garnish)

Yogurt-Dill Dressing

- ½ cup plain yogurt
- 1 small green onion, chopped
- 1½ teaspoons chopped fresh or ¼ teaspoon dried dillweed

1. Wash watercress and twist off tough stems.

2. Arrange cucumbers on plates and top with watercress. Gently mix carrot, squash, and olives and mound on top of watercress.

3. Top with a spoonful of Yogurt-Dill dressing and garnish with dill sprigs.

Yogurt-Dill Dressing Combine yogurt, green onion, and dill; chill.

COLD-WEATHER WARMUP

Mexican Bean Soup
Fruited Green Salad
Beverage suggestion:
Sangría or Rioja Blanco

Mexican Bean Soup is quick and filling—perfect for a cold, hungry crowd. Serve it accompanied with a choice of sour cream or plain yogurt, chopped cilantro, green onion, diced avocado, grated cheese, and salsa to add as toppings. The flavors of Fruited Green Salad are Mexican-inspired as well.

COOKING PLAN

1. *Assemble all ingredients and cooking equipment.*

2. *Dice vegetables for soup and sauté.*

3. *Prepare salad and dressing.*

4. *Add remaining ingredients to soup.*

5. *Chop toppings for soup and place in small bowls.*

To Serve *Place toppings for soup on table. Dress salad. Ladle soup into bowls.*

MEXICAN BEAN SOUP

 2 tablespoons butter
 ¼ cup chopped red or yellow onion
 2 carrots, diced
 2 medium zucchini, cubed
 1 can (16 oz) spicy pinto or refried beans
 1 can (14½ oz) chicken broth
 1 whole cooked chicken breast, diced
 Cilantro (*for garnish*)
 Choice of toppings: salsa, grated Cheddar cheese, chopped avocado, sour cream with chopped chives

1. In a large pot, melt butter. Add onion, carrots, and zucchini and sauté until tender (6 to 8 minutes).

2. Add beans, broth, and chicken and simmer 10 minutes.

3. Garnish with cilantro and serve with choice of toppings.

FRUITED GREEN SALAD

 1 head butter lettuce
 Half a head romaine lettuce
 6 large radishes, 6 large mushrooms, and 1 avocado, all sliced
 1 large tomato, cut in wedges
 3 peaches, peeled and sliced
 Grated Cheddar cheese (*for garnish*)

Mexican Dressing

 ½ cup mild or hot taco sauce
 ¼ cup each *red wine vinegar and salad oil*
 1 tablespoon each *diced green chiles and minced parsley*
 1 teaspoon each *minced cilantro and minced fresh oregano*

Wash lettuce, tear in bite-sized pieces, and put in large salad bowl. Top with vegetables and fruit. Toss with Mexican Dressing; garnish with cheese.

Mexican Dressing Combine taco sauce, vinegar, oil, chiles, parsley, cilantro, and oregano.

95

Tasty, filling, and nutritious breakfast sandwiches, such as this Tropical Ham Sandwich (page 101), can be enjoyed at home or on the go.

Breakfast & Brunch, Lunch & Dessert

The concept of the 30-minute meal does not apply only to dinner. In this chapter you'll find recipes for economical, nutritious breakfasts and lunches, using mostly fresh ingredients, that serve four people and can be prepared in anywhere from 5 to 25 minutes. There are also four brunch menus that have been tested for 30-minute preparation, as well as a collection of simple but special desserts, designed to create maximum appeal with minimum effort.

Serve these energizing fruit shakes as a breakfast-in-a-glass (or commuter cup) for a super start to the day, or as a nutritious after-school snack.

QUICK BREAKFASTS

Breakfast provides a foundation for the morning's jobs. Nutritionists claim that a healthy breakfast keeps you moving efficiently throughout the day. Even if you are cutting calories, you are entitled to at least a fourth of the amount allotted for your whole day at breakfast. A good morning meal may help you cut down on lunch and in-between snacks as well. The quality of breakfast depends on the food you choose. Use foods from each of the basic four food groups to make nutritious choices. Health experts suggest that breakfast include foods from at least three of these four food groups: fruits and vegetables; meat and other proteins; dairy products; and breads and cereals.

A tasty breakfast can take many forms. Try a breakfast shake or bowl of fruit soup if traditional breakfasts bore you. And fast-food restaurant sandwiches can't compare—in either speed, taste, or nutrition—with the delicious versions you can make in just 15 minutes at home.

MIX-AND-MATCH INGREDIENTS FOR FAST FRUIT SHAKES

Select one ingredient from each category, in the amount specified. You can use two ingredients from the same category (such as peaches and pineapple), each in half the amount specified for that category. You can also omit one category and double the proportions of another, to create an extra-creamy or extra-fruity shake. Add ice for quick chilling. Use frozen or canned fruits when fresh are unavailable.

Fruits (½ cup)	Dairy Products (¼ cup)	Juice (¼ cup)	Flavorings (¼ to ½ tsp or to taste)	Nutritious Additions (1 tsp)
Apples	Buttermilk	Apple	Brown sugar	Brewer's yeast
Apricots	Cottage cheese	Carrot	Cinnamon	Carob powder
Bananas	Cream cheese	Coconut	Ginger	High-protein powder
Berries	Egg, whole	Cranberry	Grape jelly	Nonfat dry milk
Dates	Ice cream, ice milk,	Grapefruit	Honey	Nuts
Kiwi fruit	or frozen yogurt	Orange	Instant coffee	Peanut butter
Mandarin	Milk: skim, whole,	Papaya	Lemon juice	Sesame or sunflower
oranges	or nonfat dry	Pineapple	Nutmeg	seed
Melons	Yogurt: plain or flavored		Orange marmalade	Wheat germ
Mangoes			Vanilla or almond extract	
Papayas				
Peaches				
Pineapples				

BREAKFAST SHAKES

Fast fruit shakes lend themselves to experimentation. To get started, use these recipes as guides. Then consult the chart for the many options fruit shakes offer. Don't forget the "nutritious additions" for an energy boost. The amounts given are for 1 serving, but the measurements can easily be doubled. To make more than two servings, make additional batches.

Prepare the fruit shakes by simply blending or processing all ingredients until smooth. Garnish with mint sprigs or fresh fruit.

Preparation Time 5 to 8 minutes

BASIC FAST FRUIT SHAKE

½ cup sliced peaches
¼ cup orange, apple, or cranberry juice
¼ teaspoon ground cinnamon
¼ cup plain low-fat yogurt or skim milk
¼ teaspoon lemon juice
½ teaspoon brown sugar or honey
2 to 3 ice cubes

Variations For the peaches, substitute ½ cup chopped cantaloupe or ½ cup drained mandarin orange segments.

ORANGE-BANANA CREAM

½ cup each orange juice and vanilla ice cream or milk
1 tablespoon creamy or chunky peanut butter
Half a small, ripe banana, quartered
Orange marmalade, to taste (for a sweeter shake)
3 ice cubes

CAROB SHAKE

½ cup vanilla, carob, or coffee ice cream
Half a banana, quartered
1 to 2 tablespoons dates and nuts of your choice
1½ tablespoons carob powder
1 egg

FRUIT NOG

¾ cup fruit of your choice
2 tablespoons frozen orange juice concentrate
¼ cup skim milk
1 tablespoon honey
¼ teaspoon vanilla extract
1 egg
2 or 3 ice cubes

Colorful, unusual, and beautiful, fruit soups are a refreshing change from routine breakfast juices. Easily puréed in a blender, they can range from savory to sweet, depending on the ingredients. Serve in glass bowls or melon shells as a delightful addition to a weekend brunch.

FRUIT SALADS AND SOUPS

Especially in the summer, fruit makes a refreshing breakfast. Here are a few out-of-the-ordinary ideas. For a complete meal, add toast and your choice of beverage.

Preparation Time 10 to 20 minutes

BREAKFAST SALAD

Combine 1 unpeeled apple, chopped; ⅓ cup *each* pumpkin *or* sunflower seeds and raisins; ¼ cup *each* chopped dates and dried apricots; and 1 banana, sliced. Serve over cottage cheese or yogurt mixed with honey to taste; or in melon halves or as a topping for hot or cold whole-grain cereal.

BERRY SOUP

   1 tablespoon unflavored gelatin
   ¼ cup cold water
   1¼ cups orange juice
   1 tablespoon lemon juice
   1 tablespoon kirsch (optional)
   1 pint each *fresh* or *1 package (10 oz) each frozen raspberries and strawberries*
   Fresh mint leaves (for garnish)

1. Soak gelatin in the water.

2. Warm orange juice and dissolve gelatin in it.

3. Place in a blender or food processor with lemon juice, kirsch (if used), and berries; blend; and chill.

4. Serve in glass bowls; garnish with mint leaves.

Variation Substitute 2 pints fresh or 1 bag (20 oz) frozen blueberries for the raspberries and strawberries.

DONNA'S MELON SOUP

Halve and seed 2 chilled cantaloupes or honeydew melons. Scoop out fruit, reserving shells, and purée in a blender (a little at a time) or a food processor. Season with a little lemon or lime juice and nutmeg or ginger. Spoon back into melon shells. Swirl a spoonful of sour cream into soup. Garnish with mint leaves.

Melon-Berry Soup Add 1 cup strawberries, raspberries, or blueberries (if you're using honeydew) to melon. Blend or process.

Peachy Melon Soup Add half a 20-ounce bag frozen sliced peaches and 1 to 2 teaspoons almond or vanilla extract to melon. Blend or process.

Tropical Fruit Soup Add 1 papaya, peeled, seeded, and chopped, and the grated rind of 1 orange and 1 lemon to cantaloupe. Blend or process. Garnish with chopped candied ginger.

FRESH FRUIT SOUP

Purée any chopped fresh fruit (peel if skin is tough) or whole berries in a blender or food processor. Thin to desired consistency by adding a complementary fruit juice or a few ice cubes. Sweeten with a little honey or sugar if desired.

For variety, try one of the fruit combinations below.

☐ Pitted cherries (quick to do if you have a pitter) or plums thinned with pomegranate juice and flavored with almond or vanilla extract.

☐ Chopped mango, papaya, and pineapple thinned with lime juice and garnished with coconut and lime wheels.

☐ Berries puréed with kiwi fruit, peaches, nectarines, or bananas. Sweeten with a little mint, currant, or cranberry jelly and swirl a spoonful of plain yogurt or sour cream into the soup. Garnish with mint leaves and lemon wheels.

BREAKFAST SANDWICHES

Try these sandwiches with juice or milk for a change of pace from eggs or cereal. Serve open-faced or topped with a second slice of toasted bread. Many of these combinations are also good for lunch. Each recipe makes 4 sandwiches.

Preparation Time 15 minutes

BROILED AVOCADO DELIGHT

Toast 4 slices whole grain bread. Layer 1 avocado, sliced; 1 cup sliced fresh mushrooms; ⅓ cup sliced almonds, toasted; and 4 slices tomato over the toast slices. Top each with a slice or two of cheese and broil until cheese melts. Garnish with olives.

BROILED VEGETABLE MIX

Sauté 1 cup sliced fresh mushrooms and ¼ cup *each* diced green or red pepper, onion, and zucchini just until softened. Distribute over 4 slices whole grain or rye toast. Top each with 1 slice Swiss cheese and a sliced ripe olive. Broil until cheese melts.

Broiled Sandwich Plus After broiling either of the preceding sandwiches, top with a fried egg. Serve open-faced.

OPEN-FACED CREAMY AVOCADO

Peel and pit 2 avocados; cut into chunks. Mix with ¼ to ½ cup sour cream, ricotta cheese, or yogurt. Mound on 4 slices whole grain toast. Sprinkle with sunflower seed if desired.

PEANUT BUTTER EXTRAVAGANZA

Toast 8 slices raisin bread. Spread 4 with ½ cup plain or chunky peanut butter; spread the other 4 with 2 bananas, mashed, or ½ cup spiced apple butter. Distribute ¼ cup each raisins, shredded coconut, and sliced almonds over peanut butter. Top with toast spread with banana. Quarter for easy eating.

TROPICAL HAM

Top buttered raisin toast with sprouts; 3 slices baked ham, rolled; 2 pineapple rings; and 1 slice Swiss cheese. Eat as is or broil to melt cheese.

BREAKFAST BLT

Mash 1 avocado with 2 tablespoons mayonnaise. Spread on 4 slices of toast. On each, layer 2 slices cooked bacon, 2 slices tomato, and a butter-lettuce leaf or a handful of alfalfa sprouts. Top with second slice of toast and quarter for easy eating.

Variation Add sliced cheese, sautéed chopped mushrooms, and chopped peppers or chiles.

SAUSAGE IN PITA

Sauté ½ pound hot or mild Italian sausage, crumbled, until browned (3 to 5 minutes). Drain off all fat. Add ¼ cup tomato sauce; 1 green pepper, chopped; half a small red onion, chopped; ½ teaspoon *each* dried oregano and basil; and 6 to 8 eggs, beaten. Cook, stirring, until eggs are set. Serve in halved pita bread.

Variation Substitute ½ cup shredded Monterey jack or mozzarella cheese for the tomato sauce.

Use basic ingredients to make nutritious breakfast sandwiches as an alternative to morning pastries. Healthy, quick, and easy to put together, breakfast sandwiches can be eaten out of hand or with a knife and fork.

QUESADILLAS

Preheat oven to 450° F. Cover the right-hand half of 4 large flour tortillas with a mixture of shredded Cheddar and Monterey jack cheese (¾ cup *each*). Top each with 1 tablespoon canned diced green chiles and a dollop of salsa (optional). You can also add sliced green or red onions and diced avocado. Fold tortillas in half; press to seal. Place on baking sheet and bake until cheese melts and tortillas are golden (5 minutes). If you'll serve them on plates, top with sour cream after baking.

Variation Fill tortillas with ¾ cup grated cheese and ¾ cup diced cooked bacon, ham, sausage, chicken, turkey, or beef. Seal and bake as directed.

CROISSANT

Sprinkle 4 croissants with a few drops of water and heat in a 350° F oven. Halve lengthwise and fill with one of the following:

☐ Omelet seasoned with herb of your choice (see page 104).

☐ Slices of ham, cheese, and pineapple.

☐ Cream cheese and a slice of smoked salmon (lox).

SEAFOOD SALAD IN PITA

Chop 6 to 8 hard-cooked eggs and mix with ¼ cup mayonnaise and about 1 cup canned salmon or other seafood. Spoon into pita bread halves and garnish with watercress leaves.

TURKEY AND FRUIT

Spread 4 slices of raisin or rye toast with spiced apple butter. Top each with sliced turkey and orange or grapefruit segments, sliced nectarines, or canned mandarin orange segments, drained.

EGG IN A HOLE

Using a round cookie cutter or the rim of a small glass, cut a circle from the center of each of 4 slices of bread. (Cut-out center may be browned in the same pan or in a toaster and served alongside.)

In a large frying pan melt 2 tablespoons butter; add bread. Crack an egg into each hole. Cook until eggs are set. Lift bread with a spatula and add 2 more tablespoons butter to pan. Flip bread over carefully and cook second side. Season with salt and pepper before serving.

FRENCH TOAST, PANCAKES, AND TOPPINGS

With this no-fuss oven-baking approach to French toast and pancakes, both can join the ranks of weekday breakfast fare. Make one of the luscious flavored toppings while breakfast bakes. Each recipe serves 4.

Preparation Time 15 minutes

OVEN-BAKED FRENCH TOAST

    4 eggs
    1 tablespoon sugar
1½ cups milk
  ¼ teaspoon nutmeg
  ½ teaspoon salt
    8 to 10 slices day-old bread
      Confectioners' sugar

1. Preheat oven to 475° F. Generously butter 2 large baking sheets.

2. In a blender or food processor, combine eggs, sugar, milk, nutmeg, and salt. Pour mixture into a shallow dish. Dip bread into egg mixture, allowing each slice to absorb as much liquid as possible.

3. Arrange slices on baking sheets and bake until golden (about 5 minutes per side).

4. Dust with confectioners' sugar, cut in half diagonally, and serve with jelly, syrup, or sour cream.

OVEN-BAKED WHEAT PANCAKES

You can substitute buckwheat, barley, oatmeal, or soy flour or wheat germ for ¼ cup of the whole wheat flour.

  2 cups buttermilk, sour milk, or orange juice
  2 eggs
  1 tablespoon brown sugar or honey
  2 cups whole wheat flour
  1 teaspoon baking soda
  ½ teaspoon salt
  1 tablespoon melted butter

1. Preheat oven to 450° F. Generously butter 2 large baking sheets and place in oven.

2. Combine buttermilk, eggs, sugar, flour, baking soda, salt, and butter. Do not overmix; it should be lumpy.

3. Ladle pancakes onto hot baking sheets and bake 10 minutes. You do *not* need to turn pancakes.

Makes 1 dozen pancakes.

ZESTY SYRUPS

Start with 2 cups purchased syrup.

Orange Add grated rind of half an orange, and ⅓ cup orange juice *or* ¼ cup Cointreau.

Gingered Add ⅓ cup orange juice and 1 tablespoon finely grated fresh ginger root *or* 1 teaspoon ground ginger.

Lemon Add lemon juice to taste (start with 2 tablespoons) and grated rind of half a lemon.

FLAVORED WHIPPED CREAM

Whip ½ pint (1 cup) whipping cream.

Maple Fold in 1 tablespoon maple syrup.

Citrus Fold in 2 teaspoons grated lime or lemon rind, some lime or lemon juice, and confectioners' sugar.

FLAVORED SOUR CREAM OR RICOTTA

Mix ½ cup *each* sour cream or ricotta cheese and plain yogurt.

Honeyed Add 1 tablespoon honey and juice and grated rind of 1 lime, 1 lemon, or half an orange.

Fruited Add 1 tablespoon favorite jelly, jam, or preserves.

Oven-Baked Wheat Pancakes (page 103), zesty toppings, and flavored butters offer unusual variations on a familiar breakfast favorite.

FLAVORED BUTTERS

Flavored butters are especially attractive when rolled in balls or formed in molds. They may be made in quantity and frozen. Thaw before serving.

Autumn Beat ¼ to ⅓ cup firmly packed brown sugar or honey, 1 teaspoon pumpkin pie spice, and ¼ to ½ cup whipping cream into 1 cup softened butter or margarine.

Fruit-Nut Beat ⅓ cup finely chopped dried dates, prunes, or apricots and 1 cup ground walnuts or pecans into 1 cup softened butter or margarine.

Honey-Nut Beat ⅓ to ½ cup honey and 2 tablespoons ground macadamia nuts, hazelnuts, or almonds into 1 cup softened butter or margarine.

OMELETS

Omelets take only a bit more time to make than scrambled eggs, but they give a more elegant effect. The technique is simple, and the possibilities for fillings practically unlimited. Allow 3 to 4 tablespoons of filling for each single-serving omelet.

Preparation Time 15 to 20 minutes for 4 single-serving omelets

BASIC SINGLE-SERVING OMELET WITH HERBS

> 3 eggs
> 1 tablespoon water
> 2 tablespoons butter
> 1 teaspoon each *minced fresh parsley, tarragon, and chives*

1. Preheat a 7- or 8-inch omelet pan over medium-high heat.

2. Mix eggs and the water with a fork until well blended but not foamy.

3. Add butter to skillet; when it foams, pour in the eggs. Slowly stir counterclockwise 3 times with a fork. Allow eggs to cook for a few seconds. Then draw eggs toward center of skillet, creating a fan effect.

4. Add herbs (or a filling of your choice; see below) and fold omelet in half with spatula. Shake pan gently, tilt over warmed serving plate, and slide omelet out. Or quickly invert with a flick of your wrist.

Mexican Sauté 2 tablespoons chopped onions in a little butter. Add diced green (mild) or jalapeño (hot) chiles, black olives, and any shredded cheese, to make a total of ¼ cup. Add to omelet in step 4 and top with a dash of salsa or a dollop of sour cream or yogurt.

Apple-Roquefort Sauté half a tart green apple, cored and thinly sliced, in 1 tablespoon butter. In step 4, add apple, grated Parmesan or shredded Monterey jack cheese, and ½ to 1 ounce Roquefort cheese. Garnish with watercress leaves.

Spinach Sauté ¼ cup chopped fresh spinach and 1 anchovy fillet, diced, in a little butter. Add to omelet in step 4; top with 1 tablespoon shredded cheese and a sprinkling of freshly grated Parmesan cheese. Garnish omelet with a fresh spinach leaf.

Provençale Sauté ¼ cup diced tomatoes and a pinch minced garlic in olive oil. Add to omelet in step 4. Sprinkle omelet with minced parsley before serving.

Princess Cook ½ cup asparagus tips; mix half with a little whipping cream. Add to omelet in step 4. Garnish with sliced raw mushrooms and remaining cooked asparagus tips.

Creole In step 2, add 1 tablespoon *each* diced tomato, onion, pimiento, and parsley plus half a clove garlic, minced, to eggs. Cook eggs as directed in step 3. Fill omelet with 2 tablespoons sautéed sliced okra or shredded sharp Cheddar cheese.

Lorraine In step 4, add 2 tablespoons *each* cooked diced bacon and shredded Gruyère or Swiss cheese, and a little chopped green onion.

Garden Patch In step 4, add ¼ cup sautéed or steamed diced mixed vegetables (leftovers are fine).

Artichoke Combine diced ham, drained chopped artichoke hearts, and shredded Muenster cheese to make a total of ¼ cup. Add to omelet in step 4.

Hearty Sauté 2 tablespoons *each* sliced chicken livers and sliced fresh mushrooms in a little butter. Add to omelet in step 4. Top with a dollop of sour cream and a sliced ripe olive.

Italian Cook 3 tablespoons crumbled Italian sausage. Add with 1 teaspoon chopped fresh *or* ¼ teaspoon dried basil to omelet in step 4. Sprinkle omelet with grated Parmesan, Romano, or Fontina cheese before serving.

Smoked Salmon In step 4, add 1 slice smoked salmon (lox), cut in strips; 2 tablespoons crumbled cream cheese; and a sprinkling of lemon juice to omelet. Sprinkle omelet with chopped chives before serving.

Once you master the omelet-making technique, you will find that the filling variations are limitless. This Hearty Omelet features mushrooms and chicken livers in the rich egg batter. Use sweet fillings to make a tasty dessert omelet.

30-MINUTE BRUNCHES

For a special weekend meal or to entertain in style, try one of these 30-minute brunch menus. Two are perfect for a luxurious late breakfast; the others are a true combination of breakfast and lunch.

BRUNCH IN THE TROPICS

Macadamia-Banana French Toast

Bacon or Sausage

Fresh Fruit Compote

Beverage suggestion:
Hawaiian Coconut Extravaganza

A banana and crushed macadamia nuts are blended into French toast batter for an unusual Hawaii-inspired brunch. For an accompaniment, try Hawaiian Coconut Extravaganza, a drink prepared and served in a coconut.

COOKING PLAN

1. Assemble all ingredients and cooking equipment.

2. Prepare fruit compote and chill.

3. Preheat oven to 475° F. Butter baking sheets. Grind nuts.

4. Prepare egg batter for French toast. Halve bread slices and coat with batter.

5. Place French toast in oven. Fry bacon or sausage.

6. Slice fruit for French toast.

To Serve *Garnish fruit compote with mint. Remove French toast from oven and top with sugar, fruit, and nuts. Drain bacon or sausage on paper towels before serving.*

MACADAMIA-BANANA FRENCH TOAST

This idea comes from a small restaurant on Maui, where fruits and nuts are served on top of waffles and French toast.

- 1 *banana, quartered*
- 4 *eggs*
- 1 *jar (3½ oz) macadamia nuts, crushed or processed*
- 1 *cup milk*
- 1 *teaspoon vanilla extract*
  Dash cinnamon or nutmeg
- 8 *to 10 slices day-old whole wheat or white bread*
  Confectioners' sugar
- 2 *bananas, sliced*

1. Preheat oven to 475° F. Generously butter 2 large baking sheets.

2. In a blender or food processor, whirl the quartered banana, eggs, half the crushed nuts, the milk, vanilla, and cinnamon until well mixed (or beat with an electric mixer).

3. Halve bread slices diagonally and arrange in a large, shallow dish. Pour egg mixture over bread, allow bread to absorb egg. Turn slices to coat other side.

4. Arrange slices on baking sheets. Bake until golden (about 5 minutes per side).

5. Remove from baking sheets and dust with confectioners' sugar. Top with banana slices and the remaining crushed nuts.

Pineapple-Coconut French Toast

Drain juice from 1 can (8 oz) crushed pineapple and add juice to egg batter in place of banana in step 2. Complete steps 3 through 5, substituting pineapple and ½ cup shredded coconut for bananas in step 5.

Papaya French Toast Follow basic recipe, but omit bananas. Top French toast with 1 papaya, sliced, and a dollop of whipped or sour cream or one of the flavored creams (recipes on page 103).

BACON OR SAUSAGE

Fry about ½ pound bacon or sausage until crisp.

FRESH FRUIT COMPOTE

Cut up a combination of fresh fruits, such as pineapple, apple, strawberries, and oranges, and chill. Serve in compotes, with a dash of Cointreau or Grand Marnier if desired, and garnish with mint sprigs.

HAWAIIAN COCONUT EXTRAVAGANZA

This refreshing drink is a striking accompaniment to the French toast. This is a bonus recipe, however: Time for its preparation is *not* included within the 30-minute cooking plan.

- 4 *coconuts*
- 4 *generous jiggers rum*
- 4 *tablespoons each orange-flavored liqueur and coconut cream*
- 3 *cups crushed ice*

1. Saw off (and reserve) the tops of the coconuts. (The hole should be about 1 inch in diameter.)

2. Add one fourth of the rum, liqueur, coconut cream, and ice to each coconut.

3. Cover holes with reserved tops and shake to mix. Provide straws for sipping.

ELEGANT SPRINGTIME BRUNCH

*Individual Cheese Soufflés
en Surprise*

Lemon-Butter Asparagus

*Wine suggestion:
Chardonnay*

Individual soufflés with an onion-mushroom filling and buttery asparagus are a fine treat on a Sunday morning in the spring. Complete the menu with croissants and an assortment of fresh fruits.

COOKING PLAN

1. *Assemble all ingredients and cooking equipment.*

2. *Chop vegetables for soufflé filling; sauté.*

3. *Preheat oven to 425° F.*

4. *Separate eggs and grate cheeses for soufflé. Beat whites and yolks.*

5. *Combine soufflé ingredients and fill soufflé dishes. Bake.*

6. *Wash asparagus and fruit. Pat fruit dry and arrange in basket.*

7. *Heat water for asparagus; cook.*

8. *Melt butter for asparagus; add lemon juice.*

To Serve *Place fruit basket on table. Drain asparagus and top with lemon butter. Serve soufflés.*

INDIVIDUAL CHEESE SOUFFLÉS EN SURPRISE

Filling

1	teaspoon butter
½	cup chopped fresh mushrooms
2	to 3 tablespoons minced green or red onion
1	tablespoon minced parsley
¼	teaspoon each *dried basil and thyme*

Soufflé

6	eggs, separated
2	tablespoons Cognac or brandy
¼	teaspoon dry mustard
¼	teaspoon each *ground nutmeg and cayenne*
1	cup ricotta cheese
¾	cup each *grated Parmesan and Swiss cheese*

1. *To prepare filling,* in medium skillet over medium-high heat, melt butter. Add mushrooms, onion, parsley, basil, and thyme. Sauté until vegetables are tender and juices are almost evaporated. Set aside.

2. Preheat oven to 425° F.

3. *To prepare soufflé,* with an electric mixer beat egg whites on high speed until they hold a stiff peak.

4. In separate bowl beat egg yolks well; add Cognac, mustard, nutmeg, cayenne, ricotta, and grated cheeses, and combine thoroughly. Stir one third of whites into yolk mixture. Fold in remaining whites.

5. Fill each of four 1-cup soufflé dishes half full of soufflé mixture, add one fourth of the mushroom filling, and top with remainder of soufflé mixture. Bake until puffed and golden (15 to 20 minutes). Serve at once.

LEMON-BUTTER ASPARAGUS

1½	to 2 pounds asparagus
2	tablespoons melted butter
1	tablespoon lemon juice
	Lemon wheels *(for garnish)*
	Grated Parmesan cheese *(for garnish; optional)*

1. Wash asparagus and cut or snap off tough ends.

2. In a wide frying pan in a little boiling salted water, lay spears parallel, no more than 3 layers deep. Cook, uncovered, over high heat until stems are just tender when pierced with a fork (6 to 8 minutes). Drain.

3. Mix butter and lemon juice. Pour over asparagus; garnish with lemon wheels and Parmesan (if used).

*Eggs in Puff Pastry
With Crab Fondue*

*Wine suggestion:
Champagne*

*Here is a brunch dish that
can wait for up to an hour:
The crab fondue can be
kept over very low heat, and
the eggs will stay moist
and warm on a warming
tray. Serve this rich entrée
with simple tomato and
avocado slices sprinkled
with dill and dressed with
oil and vinegar, and offer
fresh berries with one of
the flavored creams on
page 103.*

COOKING PLAN

1. *Assemble all ingredients and
cooking equipment.*
2. *Bake pastry shells if frozen.*
3. *Grate cheese for fondue. Prepare
and keep warm.*
4. *Cook eggs and keep warm.*

To Serve *Assemble egg-filled shells
and top with fondue, or let diners
assemble their own.*

EGGS IN PUFF PASTRY WITH CRAB FONDUE

Crab Fondue

- 2 *tablespoons* each *butter
  and flour*
- ¼ *teaspoon* each *salt and
  cayenne*
- 1¼ *cups milk*
- ¼ *cup* each *dry white wine
  or Champagne and freshly
  grated Parmesan cheese*
- 6 *to 8 ounces thawed frozen
  or canned crabmeat, drained
  and flaked*

Scrambled Eggs

- 5 *teaspoons butter*
- 2 *teaspoons flour*
- 3 *tablespoons* each *plain yogurt
  and sour cream*
- 8 *to 10 eggs*
- 4 *baked puff pastry shells*
- ¼ *cup minced parsley*

1. *To prepare fondue,* in a chafing
dish or saucepan over medium-high
heat, melt butter. Tilt dish and stir in
flour, salt, and cayenne. Blend well.

2. Add milk slowly, stirring briskly
with a wooden spoon or wire whisk.
Cook over medium heat, stirring constantly, until mixture boils and
thickens.

3. Stir in wine, cheese, and crab;
heat through. Keep warm.

4. *To prepare scrambled eggs,* in a
small saucepan melt 2 teaspoons of
the butter. Stir in flour and cook until
bubbly. Remove from heat and blend
in yogurt and sour cream. Return to
heat and cook, stirring, until bubbly
and smooth; set aside.

5. Beat eggs lightly. In a wide frying
pan, melt remaining butter. Pour in
eggs and allow to set. Run spatula
around edge, lifting to allow un-
cooked eggs to flow underneath until
eggs are softly set.

6. Remove from heat and gently stir
in yogurt-sour cream mixture. Eggs
can be served immediately or kept
warm for up to 1 hour.

7. *To serve,* spoon eggs into pastry
shells. Top with fondue. Garnish with
parsley.

PATIO BRUNCH

German Puffed Apple Pancake

Sausages

Wine suggestion:
Champagne

While you set the table, the German pancake puffs in your oven. You can vary the fruit topping by substituting other seasonal fruits, such as banana and papaya slices, for the apples. The pancake can also be a dramatic dessert, topped with Cognac and served aflame.

COOKING PLAN

1. *Assemble all ingredients and cooking equipment.*

2. *Slice apples.*

3. *Melt butter for pancake in 450° F oven. Prepare pancake batter and bake.*

4. *Fry sausages. Prepare apple topping.*

5. *Cut lemon into wedges.*

To Serve *Remove pancake from oven, top with apples, and garnish. Serve with sausages.*

GERMAN PUFFED APPLE PANCAKE

Pancake

  2 *tablespoons butter*
  3 *eggs*
  ¾ *cup* each *milk and flour*
  ¼ *to ½ teaspoon salt*

Topping

  2 *tablespoons butter*
  1 *pound tart apples, cored and thinly sliced*
  3 *to 4 tablespoons sugar*
  ⅛ *teaspoon* each *ground cinnamon and nutmeg*

Garnishes

  Confectioners' sugar and lemon wedges

1. *To prepare pancake,* melt butter in a heavy 12-inch frying pan in 450° F oven.

2. In a blender or food processor, mix eggs, milk, flour, and salt until smooth, adding one by one.

3. Pour batter into frying pan, return to oven, and bake 15 minutes. As pancake cooks, it will puff and large bubbles may form. Check periodically and pierce bubbles with a fork or toothpick.

4. *To prepare topping,* in a large frying pan over medium-high heat, melt butter. Add apples and sauté briefly. Add sugar and spices; sauté until apples are tender-crisp (6 to 8 minutes).

5. When pancake is done, remove from oven and spoon topping into center. Sprinkle with confectioners' sugar.

6. Slice pancake in wedges and serve at once, garnished with lemon wedges. Guests squeeze lemon wedges onto individual servings for piquant tart-sweet flavor.

Note For a dramatic dessert, top pancake with warmed Cognac and ignite it.

SAUSAGES

Fry 4 to 8 sausages until crisp.

LUNCH IN MINUTES

Simple purchased foods and insulated containers and bags make mix-on-the-spot meals and snacks possible. A carton of yogurt or cottage cheese and a container of cut-up fresh fruit or frozen berries can be mixed together at the office or at school for speedy nourishment. Whole fresh fruit or melon wedges, cheese, and crackers make a satisfying yet light breakfast or afternoon snack.

Use frozen foods as natural coolers for lunches that must travel. Sandwiches without mayonnaise in the filling can be prepared ahead, frozen in individual bags, and added to the lunchbox straight from the freezer. They will defrost by mealtime and will also keep other lunchbox items cool. The same approach can be used for cold soups.

LUNCHEON SOUPS

Soup, whether hot or cold, makes a complete and nutritious lunch with a roll and salad or some fruit. Lightweight, nonbreakable plastic containers that keep foods hot or cold—as well as the traditional vacuum bottle—also make it possible for soup to be the main course for a lunch away from home. As these recipes prove, soups need not be simmered for hours. They can be prepared in 8 to 25 minutes using a food processor or a blender. Each recipe makes 4 servings.

COLD CREAM OF AVOCADO SOUP

    1 large, ripe avocado, peeled,
      seeded, and coarsely chopped
      Half a medium onion,
      coarsely chopped
    3 tablespoons plain yogurt
    1½ cups chilled chicken broth
    ½ cup whipping cream
      or buttermilk
    3 or 4 dashes Worcestershire
      sauce or dry sherry
    ⅛ teaspoon freshly ground
      white pepper
      Chopped chives or chervil
      (for garnish)

In a blender or food processor, whirl avocado, onion, yogurt, broth, whipping cream, Worchestershire, and pepper until smooth. Serve immediately or chill. Garnish with chives before serving.

Preparation Time 8 minutes

Variation Add 1 clove garlic, peeled, before processing. Stir in 1 can (6 oz) shrimp or clams, drained, before serving.

COLD CURRIED APPLE SOUP

    1 tablespoon butter
    1 large red onion, sliced
    1 unpeeled apple, cored and
      sliced
    1 tablespoon curry powder
    ¼ cup flour
    2 cans (14½ oz each) chicken
      broth
    1 cup whipping cream
    2 egg yolks
      Salt, pepper, and lemon
      juice to taste
    1 unpeeled apple, cored, diced,
      and tossed with a little lemon
      juice
      Watercress sprigs (for
      garnish)

1. In a large, covered saucepan over low to medium heat, melt butter. Add onion and sliced apple and cook just until tender (about 5 minutes).

2. Add curry powder and flour, blend well, and cook until bubbly.

3. Add broth and bring to a boil. Reduce heat and simmer 5 minutes.

4. Mix cream and egg yolks. Stir a little hot soup into the cream-yolk mixture, and add it to the hot soup. Simmer until thickened. Do *not* boil or egg yolk will curdle.

5. Process or blend soup until smooth. Season and chill.

6. Before serving, stir in diced apple. Garnish with watercress.

Preparation Time 20 to 25 minutes

BLENDER BORSCHT

If you start with cold beets and broth, this soup will not need to be chilled further before serving.

    1 can (16 oz) sliced beets,
      drained
    1 can (14½ oz) chicken broth
    ¼ cup coarsely chopped onion
    1 clove garlic
    1 tablespoon lemon juice
    2 teaspoons sugar
    ½ cup sour cream or plain
      yogurt
    1 cucumber, peeled and coarsely
      chopped (optional)
    1 tablespoon fresh or ½ tea-
      spoon dried dillweed or fennel
      Chopped hard-cooked egg
      (for garnish)

1. In a blender or food processor, combine beets, broth, onion, garlic, lemon juice, and sugar. Whirl until thoroughly mixed.

2. Stir in sour cream, cucumber (if used), and dill. Garnish with chopped hard-cooked egg.

Preparation Time 8 minutes

Low-calorie Cream of Any Vegetable Soup contains no cream—nonfat dry milk helps thicken the roux. Once the base is made, add any puréed vegetable for both color and nutrition. For a finishing touch, stir 1 tablespoon of Champagne or sherry into each serving.

CORN AND CHEDDAR CHEESE CHOWDER

- 2 *tablespoons butter*
- 1 *medium onion, chopped*
- ½ *cup sliced celery*
- ¼ *cup flour*
- 1 *quart milk (at room temperature)*
- 1 *package (10 oz) frozen corn or 1 can (17 oz) cream-style or whole-kernel corn*
- 1 *can (16 oz) sliced potatoes*
- ½ *to 1 cup shredded sharp Cheddar cheese*
  Salt, freshly ground pepper, and paprika
- 2 *strips bacon, cooked and crumbled (for garnish)*

1. In a large pot, melt butter. Add onion and celery; sauté just until tender (about 5 minutes).

2. Blend in flour and cook until bubbly. Add milk and bring to a boil, stirring occasionally until thickened.

3. Add corn, potatoes, and cheese, and heat through (5 minutes). Season to taste. Garnish with crumbled bacon before serving.

Preparation Time 15 minutes

CREAM OF ANY VEGETABLE SOUP

Use this cream soup base to make soup from whatever vegetable is in season. Some possibilities are given here, or try your favorite vegetable or a combination. The soup can be served hot or chilled.

> ¼ cup butter
> 1 medium onion, thinly sliced, or 1 bunch green onions, sliced
> 2 tablespoons each *flour and non-instant, nonfat dry milk*
> 1 quart whole milk, at room temperature

1. In a large pot, melt butter. Add onion and sauté until softened.

2. Stir in flour and dry milk and cook until bubbly.

3. Gradually add whole milk, stirring until soup is smooth. Heat, stirring occasionally, until soup thickens.

4. Add your choice of vegetable (see recipes below).

5. In a blender or food processor, whirl until smooth. Serve hot or chilled.

Preparation Time 20 to 25 minutes

Cream of Lettuce In step 4, add 3 to 4 cups shredded iceberg lettuce. Cook, covered, for 3 minutes. After processing, stir in dry sherry to taste (optional). Sprinkle with paprika or nutmeg.

Cream of Broccoli Coarsely chop 1 pound broccoli. Add to soup in step 4 and simmer until tender (6 to 8 minutes). After processing, add dry sherry to taste (optional).

Cream of Mushroom In the basic recipe, replace 2 cups of the whole milk with 1 can (14½ oz) chicken or beef broth. In step 4, add 1 pound (40 medium) mushrooms, sliced or chopped, and ¼ cup chopped parsley. Cook, covered, until mushrooms are soft (about 5 minutes). After processing, stir in 1 cup plain yogurt or sour cream. Sprinkle with nutmeg.

Cream of Watercress Remove stalks from 3 bunches watercress. Add to soup in step 4. Cook, covered, for 3 minutes. After processing, garnish each serving with a dash of nutmeg and a slice of lemon.

Cream of Spinach Remove stems from 2 bunches fresh spinach and coarsely chop leaves (or thaw two 10-ounce packages frozen chopped spinach). Add to soup in step 4 and simmer 3 minutes. After processing, season with ¼ teaspoon dried thyme and stir in 1 cup plain yogurt. Garnish with sieved egg yolk.

Cream of Carrot Scrub 8 to 10 carrots; slice. Add to soup in step 4 and simmer until tender (10 to 12 minutes). After processing, stir in 1 to 2 teaspoons dried dillweed.

Cream of Asparagus Remove tough stem ends from 1 pound asparagus. Cut spears into 1-inch pieces. Add asparagus and ½ cup chopped celery to soup in step 4 and simmer until tender (5 to 7 minutes). After processing, add dry sherry to taste (optional).

Cream of Cauliflower Coarsely chop 1 medium head cauliflower. Add to soup in step 4 and simmer just until tender (10 minutes). After processing, stir in ½ cup shredded Cheddar cheese.

SEAFOOD TUREEN

> 1 tablespoon butter
> 1 pound mixed fish fillets (red snapper, sea bass, cod, sole, or salmon), cut in chunks
> 1½ cups dry white wine
> 1 cup cooked small shrimp
> 1 cup lobster meat (optional, but if omitted, add 1 cup other fish)
> ¼ pound (10 medium) mushrooms, sliced
> 1 can (16 oz) whole tomatoes, diced, and juice or 1 can (14½ oz) chicken broth
> 1 or 2 cloves garlic, minced
> ⅛ teaspoon saffron or ¼ teaspoon turmeric
> ¼ cup dry sherry (optional) Salt and freshly ground pepper

1. In a large pot, melt butter. Add fish fillets and wine. Cover and simmer just until fish becomes opaque (5 to 8 minutes).

2. Add shrimp, lobster (if used), mushrooms, tomatoes, garlic, and saffron and simmer 5 minutes.

3. Stir in sherry if desired. Season to taste.

Preparation Time 15 minutes

Variation In step 1 add ¼ to ½ cup *each* diced celery and carrot with the fish fillets.

Twelve noon doesn't have to mean tuna or peanut-butter-and-jelly on white bread. Surprise brown-baggers with specialties such as the Nut-Mushroom Spread, Carrot-Cauliflower Spread (page 116), Home-made Nut Butter, or Sugar Pea–Sesame Spread shown here, served on whole grain bread, bagels, baguettes, or pitas. The spreads can double as dips for raw vegetables, chips, or bread sticks at a party buffet. See recipes beginning on this page.

SANDWICH IDEAS

Alleviate lunchtime boredom with a bit of imagination. To make the standard sandwich more appealing, combine fillings and condiments in new ways, substitute other greens or sprouts for lettuce, and use a variety of breads and rolls—or make a sandwich without bread. With vegetable sticks, fruit, and one of the No-Bake Cookies (page 121), a sandwich becomes a part of a hearty and satisfying midday meal.

Preparation Time 10 to 15 minutes

HOMEMADE NUT BUTTERS

Nut butters are easy to prepare in a blender or food processor. Use salted or unsalted almonds, cashews, walnuts, or pecans—or combine types. For each cup of nuts, add 1 to 3 tablespoons salad oil while processing. Try one of the sandwich combinations below.

☐ Nut butter, honey, and sliced mango or papaya.

☐ Nut butter, honey, and bananas or coconut.

☐ Nut butter, spiced apple butter, and diced or grated apple.

☐ Nut butter, spiced apple butter, and trail mix.

☐ Nut butter, applesauce, wheat germ, and raisins.

STUFFED SANDWICHES

Fill hollowed-out French rolls or halved pita bread with any of these fillings.

☐ Curried Tuna and Fruit Salad (page 116).

☐ Almond Chicken or Turkey Salad or a variation (page 116).

☐ Diced cooked sausage, chopped mushrooms, and diced celery mixed with mayonnaise and mustard.

☐ Ratatouille.

☐ Guacamole (avocado mashed with lemon juice, onion, and a little hot salsa), sliced tomato, onion, olives, and spinach or lettuce leaves.

☐ Equal parts ground ham and crushed pineapple mixed with mayonnaise and Dijon mustard to taste.

☐ Deviled ham seasoned with horse-radish and a few capers.

☐ Equal parts shredded Swiss or Monterey jack cheese and chopped walnuts, diced carrot and celery, and mayonnaise and mustard to taste.

ROLL-UP SANDWICHES

Sandwiches don't necessarily have to include bread. Try some of these ideas. All should be secured with a toothpick after rolling.

☐ Wrap any sandwich filling in a lettuce or cabbage leaf.

☐ Roll beef, ham, or turkey around a dill or sweet pickle spear.

☐ Roll sliced cheese around a carrot or celery stick.

SPREADS

For those who like a light lunch, or as an accompaniment for soup or a salad of meat or seafood, these vegetable mixtures can't be beat. Serve them as dips for raw vegetables or as spreads for crackers or bread. They also make tasty vegetarian sandwich fillings.

Preparation Time 15 to 20 minutes

SUGAR PEA-SESAME SPREAD

¼ cup sesame seed
2 tablespoons butter
1 onion, thinly sliced
1 or 2 cloves garlic, minced
10 ounces fresh or 1 package (10 oz) frozen sugar peas, thawed
¼ cup sherry
2 teaspoons lemon juice
Salt and freshly ground pepper

1. In a large frying pan over medium heat, toast sesame seed, shaking pan frequently (about 5 minutes). Remove from pan.

2. Add butter and melt. Add onion and garlic and sauté until onion is limp. Add peas, sherry, and lemon juice and cook until peas are tender-crisp (about 5 minutes).

3. Process or blend until smooth. Add sesame seed; season to taste.

Makes about 2½ cups.

NUT-MUSHROOM SPREAD

4 teaspoons butter
1 package (10 oz) whole blanched almonds
1 small onion, quartered
1 or 2 cloves garlic, peeled
¾ pound (30 medium) mushrooms, halved
½ teaspoon salt
¼ teaspoon dried thyme or tarragon
¼ cup yogurt or sour cream
1 to 2 tablespoons dry sherry (optional)

1. In a frying pan, melt 1 teaspoon of the butter. Add almonds and toast, shaking pan occasionally (about 5 minutes). Remove from pan.

2. Meanwhile, process or blend onion and garlic with short on-off pulses until coarsely chopped. Remove from container; process or blend mushrooms in the same way.

3. Melt remaining butter in pan. Add onions, garlic, mushrooms, salt, and thyme. Cook over medium-high heat, shaking pan occasionally, until most of the juices have evaporated.

4. Reserving ½ cup of the almonds, process or blend the remainder until finely ground.

5. Add vegetables (and any juices) and yogurt to container with nuts and process until almost smooth. Add sherry (if used) to taste.

6. Place in bowl or terrine, garnish with reserved almonds, cover, and chill.

Makes about 3 cups.

CARROT-CAULIFLOWER SPREAD

1 tablespoon butter
1 small onion, sliced
1 or 2 cloves garlic, minced
1 cup each *thinly sliced carrot and cauliflower*
½ teaspoon each *curry powder and salt*
⅔ cup water
1 cup salted cashews or peanuts
1½ to 2 tablespoons oil

1. In a large skillet melt butter. Add onion and garlic and sauté until onion is soft. Add carrot, cauliflower, curry powder, and salt and sauté briefly.

2. Add the water, cover skillet, and bring liquid to a boil. Reduce heat and simmer 6 to 8 minutes.

3. Meanwhile, in a blender or food processor, finely grind ¾ cup of the nuts. Gradually add oil, processing continuously until mixture is creamy and smooth.

4. Add vegetables and process until smooth. Stir in the remaining ¼ cup nuts, coarsely chopped.

5. Serve at room temperature or chill.

Makes about 2 cups.

SALADS AND DRESSINGS

Whether a mixture of greens and chopped vegetables or a more substantial combination that includes meat or seafood, salads are lunchtime favorites. They are also a perfect way to make use of small amounts of leftovers. Salads can include cooked vegetables marinated in a little vinegar and oil, slices or wedges of hard-cooked eggs, flaked fish or chopped meat, fresh or canned fruit, and cheeses of all kinds. With bread or a roll and perhaps a light soup, you have a filling meal.

Salads make good box or bag lunches as long as you pack the dressing, the greens, and the meat or fish mixture separately. Insulated plastic containers will keep everything cool until lunchtime.

The two quick meat and seafood salads can also be used as sandwich fillings. All recipes serve 4.

Preparation Time 5 to 15 minutes

CURRIED TUNA AND FRUIT SALAD

¼ cup each *mayonnaise and plain yogurt*
2 tablespoons lemon juice
1 to 2 tablespoons curry powder
1 tablespoon chutney, chopped
2 cans (6½ oz each) *chunk-style tuna, drained*
1 cup thinly sliced celery
¼ cup thinly sliced green onion
2 apples, cored and diced
1 cup seedless grapes or raisins
Shredded coconut and almonds (*for garnish*)

Combine mayonnaise, yogurt, lemon juice, curry powder, and chutney thoroughly. Gently mix in tuna, celery, green onion, apples, and grapes. Garnish with shredded coconut and almonds.

SUMMER SALAD

4 peaches, sliced
2 pears, sliced and dipped in lemon juice
Half a pineapple, cut in chunks
1 pint fresh strawberries
12 cooked medium-sized shrimp
8 slices baked or boiled ham, rolled
Lettuce leaves

Watercress Mayonnaise Dip

1 bunch watercress, (stems removed), coarsely chopped
3 tablespoons lemon juice
¼ teaspoon dried tarragon
1 clove garlic, minced
1 cup mayonnaise
Sieved egg yolk (*for garnish*)

1. Arrange fruits, shrimp, and ham on lettuce leaves.

2. Serve with Watercress Mayonnaise Dip. Provide toothpicks or seafood forks for dipping.

Watercress Mayonnaise Dip In a blender or food processor, combine watercress, lemon juice, tarragon, garlic, and mayonnaise. Process until smooth. Garnish with egg yolk.

ALMOND CHICKEN OR TURKEY SALAD

1½ to 2 cups diced or shredded cooked chicken or turkey
½ cup sliced celery
¼ cup each *chopped green onion and salted almonds*
2 teaspoons each *lemon juice and Dijon mustard*
¼ teaspoon salt
¼ cup each *mayonnaise and yogurt*

Combine chicken, celery, onion, and almonds. Mix together lemon juice, mustard, salt, mayonnaise, and yogurt. Fold into meat mixture.

Walnut Substitute walnuts for the almonds and garnish with cucumber slices.

Spicy Substitute ¼ to ½ cup bottled French dressing for the mayonnaise and yogurt. Garnish with sliced pimiento, olives, hard-cooked eggs, and capers.

Fruited Reduce lemon juice to 1 teaspoon; substitute 1 teaspoon sugar for the mustard and ¼ cup sour cream for the yogurt. Add ½ cup diced apples, halved grapes, pineapple chunks, or orange segments to the meat mixture.

Oriental Substitute ½ cup sliced water chestnuts and ½ cup bean sprouts for the celery, onion, and almonds. Season mayonnaise-yogurt mixture to taste with salt, sugar, and ground coriander (start with ¼ teaspoon). (Omit lemon juice and mustard.)

This seafood, ham, and fruit–filled Summer Salad, with its tangy Watercress Mayonnaise Dip, makes a delicious finger-food lunch. Serve it with croissants or muffins when it's just too hot to cook.

117

SPICY AVOCADO DRESSING

This dressing goes well with green or citrus-and-green salads, and it makes a tasty substitute for mayonnaise in chicken or turkey salads.

- 1 cup plain yogurt or mayonnaise
- 1 ripe avocado, peeled, seeded, and coarsely chopped
- 1/3 cup lemon juice
- 2 tablespoons milk
- 1 clove garlic, crushed
- 1/2 teaspoon salt
- 1/4 teaspoon each *hot-pepper sauce* and *cumin*

In a blender or food processor, blend yogurt, avocado, lemon juice, milk, garlic, and seasonings until thoroughly combined.

CITRUS-HONEY DRESSING

This is a tasty sweet dressing for fruit salads, or for green or meat salads that contain fruit.

- 1 cup each *ricotta or cottage cheese* and *plain yogurt*
- 2 tablespoons honey
- 2 tablespoons chopped fresh mint
  Grated rind of 1 lemon and 1 lime
- 1 tablespoon each *lemon* and *lime juice*

In a blender or food processor, blend ricotta, yogurt, honey, mint, and fruit rind and juices until thoroughly combined.

Orange Dressing Substitute grated orange rind and juice for the lime.

Poppy Seed Dressing Omit the mint. Add 1 to 2 tablespoons poppy seed to dressing after blending.

Gingered Fruit Dressing Substitute 1 teaspoon freshly grated ginger root for the mint.

LEMON-LIME YOGURT DRESSING

Flavor this tangy dressing with Dijon mustard for meat salads and with dill for fish salads.

- 2 cups plain yogurt
- 1/4 cup each *lemon and lime juice*
  Yolks of 3 hard-cooked eggs
- 6 shallots, peeled, or 1/4 cup coarsely chopped green or red onion
- 1/3 cup chopped parsley
  Salt and pepper
  Whites of 3 hard-cooked eggs, chopped (optional)

In a blender or food processor, blend yogurt, fruit juices, egg yolks, shallots, parsley, and salt and pepper to taste until thoroughly combined. Stir in chopped whites if desired.

MUSTARD VINAIGRETTE DRESSING

This dressing is delicious on or mixed with green, meat, or bean salads. Vary the flavor by adding minced fresh herbs and by using flavored vinegars and olive or nut oil.

- 1 teaspoon each *salt and Dijon mustard*
- 1/4 teaspoon *freshly ground pepper*
- 1 clove garlic, crushed
- 1/4 cup *red wine vinegar*
- 2 tablespoons lemon juice
- 2/3 cup salad oil

Mix salt, mustard, pepper, garlic, and vinegar to allow the vinegar to dissolve the salt. Whisk in lemon juice and oil.

Egg Vinaigrette Whisk in yolk of a soft-boiled egg with the lemon juice; then whisk in oil. Add chopped egg white to finished dressing.

Hearty Vinaigrette Add one or a combination of the following to the basic Mustard Vinaigrette: minced shallots, chives, pimiento, or anchovy fillets; chopped cornichons or gherkins; capers.

DESSERTS: SIMPLE BUT SPECIAL

For those who like their meals to end with a flourish, here is a potpourri of quick desserts. Though preparation times vary, all are short enough for the cook in a hurry. Some of these desserts are simple variations on storebought favorites. Some are no-fuss—and relatively low-calorie—fruit-and-cheese plates. For family dinners, there are quick cookie recipes and ideas for turning a bowl of ice cream into something special. And there are also some decadently rich parfaits and mousses for entertaining or just to end an everyday meal in a spectacular way. All recipes serve four.

QUICK IDEAS FOR STORE-BOUGHT DESSERTS

Cookies, cakes, ice cream, and fruit are favorites of children and adults alike. It takes only a few minutes to make them even more inviting. A few of these desserts must be chilled briefly or frozen.

Preparation Time 5 to 10 minutes

The Big Cookie Oversized cookies (about 5 inches in diameter) are great all by themselves. But for a real treat, top a chewy chocolate chip or granola cookie with fresh fruit slices, a scoop of ice cream, chocolate sauce, whipped cream, and nuts—the cookie equivalent of the banana split.

Make-Your-Own Ice Cream Sandwiches Spoon slightly softened ice cream onto your favorite cookie (molasses or peanut butter is good); top with a second cookie and freeze.

For chocolate lovers, melt chocolate and cool to lukewarm; dip frozen sandwiches in chocolate. Refrigerate to set chocolate.

Continental Serve delicate, bite-sized cookies with sliced fruit.

Cookie Crunch Crush chewy cookies such as macaroons and mix with sliced fruit or top with a scoop of ice cream.

Cheesecake Top with sliced fresh or canned fruit, enhanced with a little liqueur if desired.

Poundcake Slice poundcake. Top with ice cream and chocolate or berry sauce, or with sliced or crushed fresh fruit.

Trifle In a clear bowl layer slices of cake or ladyfingers, sprinkled with sherry if desired. Top with crushed fruit, and pudding or fruit syrup.

Turnovers, Sweet Crêpes, and Sweet Croissants Thaw baked frozen pastries and top or fill with ice cream, flavored sour or whipped cream (see recipes on page 103) chocolate sauce, or sliced fresh fruit.

FRUIT AND CHEESE DESSERTS

Just-picked fruits at the peak of ripeness need no embellishment, but for variety, try these ideas. Don't forget cheese—it's fruit's natural partner.

Preparation Time 5 to 10 minutes

Chocolate-Covered Fruit Dip chilled whole strawberries or sliced firm fruits (pears, apples, peaches, nectarines) in melted chocolate. For variety, use dark and white chocolate, melted separately. Roll in chopped hazelnuts or pistachio nuts and refrigerate to set chocolate.

Nutty Chocolate Bananas Dip peeled bananas in melted chocolate and roll in chopped or ground nuts or coconut—or both. Refrigerate. Serve whole or in slices.

Flavored Dip for Fruit Mix together 1 cup sour cream, 1 teaspoon *each* lemon juice and grated rind, ¼

cup confectioners' sugar, a dash nutmeg, and kirsch to taste (optional). Serve in small bowls along with brown sugar and whole strawberries or sliced fruit.

Fruit and Cheese Here are some classic fruit and cheese combinations:

☐ Golden Delicious apples, bananas, and kiwi with Brie or Camembert, Stilton, and Port-du-Salut.

☐ Pears, pineapple, and tangerines with Gorgonzola, Gruyère, and Tilsit.

☐ Green grapes, pears, and strawberries with sharp Cheddar, Monterey jack, and blue.

☐ Papaya, pears, and honeydew melon with Swiss, Edam or Gouda, and a French double-cream.

For a special presentation, peel the rind from a small round of Brie. Coat cheese with brown sugar and chopped walnuts and broil until cheese begins to soften. Serve with sliced apples or fruit of your choice.

A no-fuss finale in the European tradition features a variety of cheeses in wedges, slices, or balls, served with fruits, nuts, and crackers. Offer a selection of fruit liqueurs or serve a dessert wine such as a late-harvest Zinfandel, a port, or a Muscat Canelli.

Ice Cream With Chocolate Curls

Using a grater, shave dark chocolate over scoops of rich strawberry ice cream, Italian gelato, or frozen yogurt. Garnish with a stemmed, whole berry. Or shave white chocolate over chocolate or coffee ice cream.

Parfait Crunch Layer vanilla, peppermint, or nut ice cream with crushed peppermint candy, almond bark, or peanut brittle. If you wish, you can also add a complementary liqueur. Top with whipped cream and a sprinkling of candy.

Citrus Sundae Top scoops of citrus sherbet or frozen yogurt with fresh pineapple chunks, kiwi slices, and fresh or frozen raspberries.

Continental Parfait Crush cookies (macaroons or one of the Continental cookies) and layer with ice cream. Top with whipped cream and a sprinkling of crushed cookie.

Hazelnut-Almond Parfait Alternate layers of nutted (butter pecan, for instance) or vanilla ice cream, Frangelica (hazelnut liqueur), and sliced almonds or chopped toasted hazelnuts. Top with whipped cream and a sprinkling of almonds or hazelnuts.

Springtime Sundae Pipe whipped cream around scoops of vanilla or boysenberry ice cream or frozen yogurt in wine or sherbet glasses. Top with candied violets.

Double-Coffee Sundae Top scoops of coffee ice cream with whipped cream (flavored, if you wish, with a little coffee or coffee-flavored liqueur) and candied coffee beans.

Use the ideas on this page, such as the fresh raspberry parfait shown here, to put on your own ice cream social—a great way to entertain a group of teenagers. Provide several flavors of ice cream and frozen yogurt; syrups and sauces; toppings, including chopped fruits and nuts; and lots of whipped cream. Have on hand plenty of sundae dishes, ice-cream scoops, and spoons, and don't forget the napkins!

SUNDAES AND PARFAITS

Ice cream or frozen-yogurt desserts can be simple—or you can make them festive and elegant. The combinations are limited only by your imagination.

Preparation Time 5 to 10 minutes

Toppings Try these as toppings for sundaes, or layer them with ice cream or yogurt in parfaits:

☐ Chopped nuts

☐ Shredded coconut

☐ Shaved chocolate

☐ Crushed candies

☐ Sliced or crushed fresh fruit

☐ Whole or chopped candied fruit

☐ Chopped fruits soaked in liqueur or fruit juice

☐ Granola or other crunchy cereals

☐ Maple or berry syrups

☐ Liqueurs

☐ Whipped cream

NO-BAKE COOKIES

These simple-to-make cookies can be kept in the refrigerator for up to a week, or can be frozen for longer storage. Add them to the lunch box frozen and they will have thawed by lunchtime. They're also great energizers for hiking or skiing.

Preparation Time 10 minutes

FRUIT CHEWS

  ½ cup butter
  1 cup honey
  ¼ cup carob powder
  1 cup grated apple
  ¼ teaspoon salt
  2 tablespoons wheat germ
  ½ teaspoon pumpkin pie spice
     or cinnamon
  3 cups quick-cooking oatmeal
  ½ cup each chopped dried dates
     and apricots
  ½ cup each chopped walnuts
     and flaked coconut
  1 teaspoon vanilla extract

1. In a large saucepan melt butter. Add honey, carob powder, apple, salt, wheat germ, spice, and oatmeal; stir, and heat through.

2. Add fruits, nuts, coconut, and vanilla and mix well.

3. Drop by heaping teaspoonfuls onto a buttered baking sheet or waxed paper. Refrigerate or freeze.
Makes 5 dozen cookies.

JEWEL DROPS

  1 cup each dried dates, apricots,
     prunes, and raisins
  ½ cup (4-oz pkg) chopped nuts
  1 teaspoon pumpkin pie spice
  ½ cup instant oatmeal

1. In a food processor combine dried fruit, nuts, and spice and process until blended (2 to 3 minutes).

2. Shape in walnut-sized balls and roll in cereal. Refrigerate or freeze.
Makes 3 dozen cookies.

FROZEN DESSERTS

All of these desserts are light, refreshing, and appealing to the eye. Although they must be chilled before you can serve them, they are quick and easy to prepare. Mix them up along with the rest of the meal, put them in the freezer before sitting down to eat, and most will be ready when you are. Or chill them overnight for a meal on the next day.

Where recipes call for berries, you can choose either fresh or frozen. Although fresh berries are, of course, tastiest for eating whole, their availability is limited and they can be costly. Unless you have a source of inexpensive fresh berries, don't hesitate to use the frozen ones. They produce excellent results in these desserts.

PAPAYA ICE

This sunny dessert is light and different. You can also serve it with a wedge of melon for breakfast on a hot summer morning. Fresh pineapple, mango, or peaches may be substituted for the papaya, or experiment with frozen fruits or combinations of fruits for variety.

  1 cup sugar
  1 cup water
     Juice of one lime or lemon
  4 papayas, peeled, seeded, and
     coarsely chopped
     Mint leaves (for garnish)

1. In a saucepan bring sugar and the water to a boil. Place in freezer to chill for 5 minutes.

2. Put syrup in a blender or food processor, and purée with lime juice and papaya. Pour into a shallow metal pan (for fast freezing). Freeze at least 20 minutes.

3. Serve in dessert dishes, or for a festive touch, in hollowed-out orange shells.

Note Ice may be thawed slightly before serving and beaten with an electric mixer to a creamy slush.

Preparation Time 15 minutes

Freezing Time 20 minutes

FRUIT-CREAM PARFAIT

  8 ounces cream cheese, softened
  1 cup whipping cream
  ¼ cup confectioners' sugar
  1 to 2 teaspoons lemon juice
     Grated rind of 1 orange
     and 1 lemon
 2½ cups sliced fresh or
     frozen fruit
     Whipped cream or chopped
     nuts (for garnish)

1. In an electric mixer beat cream cheese and whipping cream on high speed until light and fluffy.

2. Reduce speed to low and add sugar, lemon juice, and citrus rind.

3. Layer one eighth of the cream cheese mixture in each of 4 wineglasses. Top with ½ cup of fruit and one fourth of the remaining cream cheese. Chill in freezer 10 to 15 minutes.

4. Divide remaining ½ cup fruit among the 4 wineglasses and garnish as desired.

Preparation Time 10 minutes

Freezing Time 10 to 15 minutes

Frozen desserts range from light and refreshing to decadently rich. From left to right in front are: Chocolate Mousse and Strawberry, Raspberry, and Blueberry Fruit Mousses. Papaya Ice (page 121) is in the back.

CHOCOLATE MOUSSE

You can make this mousse ahead and refrigerate it for up to 3 days.

   8 *ounces good-quality semisweet chocolate, broken in pieces*
   1 *cup unsalted butter*
   ¼ *to ½ cup sugar (to taste)*
   6 *eggs*
   2 *to 3 tablespoons Cognac, amaretto, or concentrated coffee*
      Whipping cream, chocolate shavings, and crushed macaroons or almonds (for garnish; optional)

1. In top of double boiler or in microwave oven melt chocolate.

2. With electric mixer, beat butter and sugar at high speed until light and fluffy.

3. Add chocolate and eggs, one at a time, beating until thoroughly blended. Stir in Cognac.

4. Spoon into soufflé dish or individual serving dishes and freeze 10 minutes. Cover and refrigerate until serving.

5. Garnish if desired.

Preparation Time 10 minutes

Freezing Time 10 to 15 minutes

FRUIT MOUSSE

   3 *egg whites*
   ¼ *cup sugar*
   2 *pints fresh or 1 package (20 oz) frozen strawberries, raspberries, or blueberries, thawed and drained*
   1 *cup plain yogurt*
   1 *teaspoon vanilla or almond extract*
      Kiwi fruit, ground almond macaroons, lime wedges or slices, mint leaves, whipped cream, or whole berries (for garnish)

1. With an electric mixer beat whites at high speed until they form soft peaks. Gradually beat in sugar.

2. In a blender or food processor, purée berries with yogurt and vanilla.

3. Stir a third of egg whites into fruit mixture. Fold in remaining whites.

4. Divide mixture among 4 parfait glasses and freeze.

5. Garnish as desired before serving.

Preparation Time 15 minutes

Freezing Time 15 minutes

Variation Complete steps 1 and 2, omitting yogurt. Whip 1 cup whipping cream; fold into egg whites with fruit. In step 4 layer mousse with crushed cookies if desired. Garnish with fresh berries and lime slices.

DESSERTS FOR SPECIAL OCCASIONS

Here are some grand finales that take only 10 to 15 minutes to prepare.

FLAMING BANANAS FOSTER

You can substitute 4 large fresh peaches or pears or 2 papayas for the bananas.

⅓ *cup butter*
⅓ *cup firmly packed brown sugar or ¼ cup honey*
4 *bananas*
2 *cups praline or coffee ice cream*
3 *tablespoons each rum and banana liqueur*

1. In a medium frying pan on the stove, melt butter and sugar.

2. Slice bananas lengthwise and then crosswise into chunks. Toss gently in sauce to warm.

3. Divide ice cream among 4 parfait or wineglasses.

4. Add rum and liqueur to bananas; heat on high for 1 minute and ignite. Spoon sauce over ice cream.

Preparation Time 10 minutes

FIGS WITH FLAVORED RICOTTA

12 *medium-sized ripe fresh figs*
1 *cup ricotta cheese*
1 *teaspoon each grated lemon and orange rind*
¾ *teaspoon vanilla extract*
¼ *cup honey*
  Chopped pistachios, hazelnuts, or almonds (for garnish)

1. Remove stem ends from figs. Cut each into a tulip shape by slicing in quarters from stem *almost* to blossom end. Press on stem end to open petals.

2. In blender or food processor whirl ricotta, citrus rinds, vanilla, and honey.

3. Stuff each fig with 2 tablespoons flavored ricotta.

4. Garnish with chopped nuts.

Preparation Time 10 minutes

End your 30-minute meal with a flourish of Flaming Bananas Foster. Other fruits can be substituted for the bananas; you can also pour the delicious sauce over angel food cake.

The elegant appearance of *Rosé Pears in Chocolate Bath belies its ease of preparation. Simply poach fresh or canned pears, stuff them with dried nuts, and float them in a sea of flavored chocolate. For the finishing touch, garnish with a mint sprig.*

ROSÉ PEARS IN CHOCOLATE BATH

Poach the pears and mix the sauce ahead of time; then assemble this elegant dessert just before serving.

2½ cups burgundy wine
⅓ cup sugar
    Half a stick cinnamon, broken
⅛ teaspoon coriander seed or pinch ground coriander
3 whole cloves
    Grated rind of half an orange
    Grated rind of 1 lemon
4 Bartlett pears, peeled
1 can (5 oz) chocolate sauce

2 to 3 tablespoons Cognac, Grand Marnier, or almond liqueur
    Mint sprigs, kiwi slices, or candied violets (for garnish)

1. In a medium saucepan combine wine, sugar, cinnamon, coriander, cloves, and citrus rinds. Bring to a boil.

2. Add pears, reduce heat, and simmer just until tender (8 to 10 minutes).

3. With a slotted spoon remove pears. Halve and core if desired. Place one pear upright in each of 4 Champagne or sherbet glasses.

4. Mix chocolate sauce and Cognac. Pour around pears and garnish as desired.

Preparation Time 15 to 20 minutes

Nut-Filled Pears in Chocolate
Poach pears as directed in steps 1 and 2. Halve pears horizontally, cutting in a sawtooth pattern to flute. Core, and stuff each half with a mixture of chopped nuts, raisins, dried dates, and dried apricots. Reassemble pears and surround each one with chocolate sauce.

Rosé Pears With Vanilla Cream
Poach the pears as directed in steps 1 and 2. Mix 1 to 2 tablespoons Cognac into 1 cup vanilla pudding. Whip 1 carton (8 oz) whipping cream and fold into pudding. Place vanilla cream in bottom of serving glasses (wineglasses look elegant). Add pears and garnish with mint.

Rosé Pears and Ice Cream Poach pears as directed in steps 1 and 2. Halve vertically, and core. Place a scoop of your favorite ice cream, sherbet, or frozen yogurt in each of 4 Champagne or sherbet glasses. Lean 2 pear halves against each scoop.

FRUITED MELON MERINGUE

4 egg whites
1 tablespoon sugar
2 small honeydew melons or cantaloupes, halved and seeded
2 cups ice cream or frozen yogurt
2 peaches or pears, sliced

1. Preheat oven to 450° F.

2. With an electric mixer whip whites and sugar until stiff. Pipe or spoon in 4 mounds onto baking sheet lined with cooking parchment. Bake until meringues are lightly browned (2 to 3 minutes). Cool.

3. Place melon halves in serving bowls. Fill with ice cream; place fruit slices on top.

4. Top each melon half with a meringue.

Preparation Time 15 minutes

PEARS WITH MELBA SAUCE

For a more substantial dessert, serve these colorful pears over ice cream or slices of purchased angel food cake.

½ cup water
¼ cup granulated sugar
4 fresh pears, quartered and cored
1 pint fresh or 1 package (10 oz) frozen raspberries, thawed
2 teaspoons lemon juice
3 tablespoons confectioners' sugar (or to taste)
1 tablespoon kirsch (optional)
2 kiwi fruit, sliced (optional)

1. In a saucepan mix the water and granulated sugar. Bring to a boil over high heat, add pears, reduce heat,

and simmer until fork-tender (10 minutes). Discard poaching liquid or save for poaching other fruit.

2. Meanwhile, in blender or food processor, purée raspberries; strain if desired. Stir in lemon juice, confectioners' sugar, and kirsch (if used).

3. Remove pears to serving dish. Pour sauce over and garnish with kiwi slices if desired.

Preparation Time 15 minutes

SWEET SOUFFLÉED OMELET

¼ cup milk
4 eggs, separated
1 tablespoon each Cognac or Grand Marnier and granulated sugar
1 tablespoon butter

Topping

Confectioners' sugar
2 tablespoons orange juice
2 to 3 tablespoons Grand Marnier, warmed

1. Preheat oven to 350° F.

2. In a medium bowl combine thoroughly milk, egg yolks, Cognac, and granulated sugar with a fork.

3. In a separate bowl beat egg whites until stiff but not dry.

4. Stir one third of the whites into yolk mixture. Fold in remaining whites.

5. In an ovenproof skillet over medium-high heat, melt butter. Add batter and cover skillet. Cook five minutes, slashing once with a knife to bottom crust to permit heat to penetrate.

6. Remove lid and transfer omelet to oven until top is set (2 minutes).

7. Remove omelet from skillet; sprinkle with confectioners' sugar and orange juice. Pour warm liqueur over or around it and ignite.

Preparation Time 15 minutes

Topping Variations Substitute any of the following for the Grand Marnier topping:

☐ Apricot-pineapple preserves.

☐ Sliced fresh fruit topped with powdered sugar or honey.

☐ Whole berries and sour or whipped cream mixed with a little grated lemon rind and lemon juice.

☐ Amaretto, sliced almonds, and sweetened sour cream, whipped cream or ricotta cheese.

☐ Grand Marnier and orange slices.

BRANDIED FRUIT FLAMBÉ

Make this elegant topping for ice cream or cheesecake with any fresh fruit. It can also be served on a bed of crushed macaroons. If you don't have a chafing dish, prepare the flambé in a saucepan or frying pan.

½ cup each sugar and water
3 whole cloves
1 stick cinnamon, broken in pieces
2 cups fresh fruit, cut in bite-sized pieces
2 cups ice cream
¼ cup Cognac

1. In a chafing dish bring sugar, the water, cloves, and cinnamon to a boil; boil 5 minutes. Discard spices.

2. Add fruit and simmer until warmed through.

3. Divide ice cream among 4 parfait glasses.

4. Add Cognac to fruit, heat thoroughly and ignite, and spoon sauce over ice cream.

Preparation Time 15 minutes

INDEX

Note: Page numbers in italics refer to illustrations separated from recipe text.

U.S. MEASURE AND METRIC MEASURE CONVERSION CHART

Formulas for Exact Measures | **Rounded Measures for Quick Reference**

	Symbol	When you know:	Multiply by:	To find:			
Mass (Weight)	oz	ounces	28.35	grams	1 oz		= 30 g
	lb	pounds	0.45	kilograms	4 oz		= 115 g
	g	grams	0.035	ounces	8 oz		= 225 g
	kg	kilograms	2.2	pounds	16 oz	= 1 lb	= 450 g
					32 oz	= 2 lb	= 900 g
					36 oz	= 2¼ lb	= 1,000 g (1 kg)
Volume	tsp	teaspoons	5.0	milliliters	¼ tsp	= 1/24 oz	= 1 ml
	tbsp	tablespoons	15.0	milliliters	½ tsp	= 1/12 oz	= 2 ml
	fl oz	fluid ounces	29.57	milliliters	1 tsp	= ⅙ oz	= 5 ml
	c	cups	0.24	liters	1 tbsp	= ½ oz	= 15 ml
	pt	pints	0.47	liters	1 c	= 8 oz	= 250 ml
	qt	quarts	0.95	liters	2 c (1 pt)	= 16 oz	= 500 ml
	gal	gallons	3.785	liters	4 c (1 qt)	= 32 oz	= 1 l.
	ml	milliliters	0.034	fluid ounces	4 qt (1 gal)	= 128 oz	= 3¾ l.
Length	in.	inches	2.54	centimeters	⅜ in.	= 1 cm	
	ft	feet	30.48	centimeters	1 in.	= 2.5 cm	
	yd	yards	0.9144	meters	2 in.	= 5 cm	
	mi	miles	1.609	kilometers	2½ in.	= 6.5 cm	
	km	kilometers	0.621	miles	12 in. (1 ft)	= 30 cm	
	m	meters	1.094	yards	1 yd	= 90 cm	
	cm	centimeters	0.39	inches	100 ft	= 30 m	
					1 mi	= 1.6 km	
Temperature	° F	Fahrenheit	5/9 (after subtracting 32)	Celsius	32° F	= 0° C	
					68° F	= 20° C	
	° C	Celsius	9/5 (then add 32)	Fahrenheit	212° F	= 100° C	
Area	in.²	square inches	6.452	square centimeters	1 in.²	= 6.5 cm²	
	ft²	square feet	929.0	square centimeters	1 ft²	= 930 cm²	
	yd²	square yards	8,361.0	square centimeters	1 yd²	= 8,360 cm²	
	a	acres	0.4047	hectares	1 a	= 4,050 m²	

Proof-of-Purchase
0-89721-051-4